LEADING WITH
JOY

LEADING WITH JOY

Practices for Uncertain Times

Akaya Windwood and Rajasvini Bhansali

BK®

Berrett-Koehler Publishers, Inc.

Berrett-Koehler Publishers, Inc.
1333 Broadway, Suite 1000
Oakland, CA 94612-1921
Tel: (510) 817-2277; Fax: (510) 817-2278
www.bkconnection.com

ORDERING INFORMATION
QUANTITY SALES. Special discounts are available on quantity purchases by corporations, associations, and others. For details, contact the "Special Sales Department" at the Berrett-Koehler address above.
INDIVIDUAL SALES. Berrett-Koehler publications are available through most bookstores. They can also be ordered directly from Berrett-Koehler: Tel: (800) 929-2929; Fax: (802) 864-7626; www.bkconnection.com.
ORDERS FOR COLLEGE TEXTBOOK / COURSE ADOPTION USE. Please contact Berrett-Koehler: Tel: (800) 929-2929; Fax: (802) 864-7626.

Distributed to the U.S. trade and internationally by Penguin Random House Publisher Services.

Berrett-Koehler and the BK logo are registered trademarks of Berrett-Koehler Publishers, Inc.

Printed in the United States of America

Berrett-Koehler books are printed on long-lasting acid-free paper. When it is available, we choose paper that has been manufactured by environmentally responsible processes. These may include using trees grown in sustainable forests, incorporating recycled paper, minimizing chlorine in bleaching, or recycling the energy produced at the paper mill.

Library of Congress Cataloging-in-Publication Data
    Names: Windwood, Akaya, author. | Bhansali, Rajasvini, author.
    Title: Leading with joy : practices for uncertain times / Akaya Windwood, Rajasvini Bhansali.
    Description: First Edition. | Oakland, CA : Berrett-Koehler Publishers, [2022] | Includes index.
    Identifiers: LCCN 2022010241 (print) | LCCN 2022010242 (ebook) | ISBN 9781523002825 (paperback) | ISBN 9781523002832 (pdf) | ISBN 9781523002849 (epub) | ISBN 9781523002856
    Subjects: LCSH: Leadership—Psychological aspects. | Personnel management. | Interpersonal relations.
    Classification: LCC HD57.7 .W563 2022 (print) | LCC HD57.7 (ebook) | DDC 658.4/09—dc23/ eng/20220303
    LC record available at https://lccn.loc.gov/2022010241
    LC ebook record available at https://lccn.loc.gov/2022010242

First Edition
28 27 26 25 24 23 22 • 10 9 8 7 6 5 4 3 2 1

Book producer: BookMatters
Cover design and illustrations: Mike Nicholls
Author photograph: Heward Jue

To Jeanne Jones, and to mothers everywhere who do their best to find a way out of no way. We dedicate this book to all those who make life possible.

To Rajendra Kumar Bhansali, in honor of a life spent leading with joy and creativity for the public good. We dedicate this book to all those who believe in human potential, especially during uncertain times.

✻ CONTENTS

✱ PREFACE

Many years ago Steve Piersanti, having heard Akaya Windwood speak at a conference, approached her and asked if she had ever considered writing a book. Akaya was busy running a leadership-development organization and could not then imagine having the time or space to do a book justice. They stayed in touch, but she remained reluctant to write, despite Steve's encouragement. A few years later, Akaya and Rajasvini Bhansali were having one of their usual hangouts in the garden and Akaya said "Let's write a book." Without a moment's hesitation, Rajasvini said yes. She knew that anything Akaya invited her into would be a giant adventure filled with the opportunity to self-reflect, learn, and contribute to the world. In that moment, Akaya realized that it wasn't true that she didn't want to write a book, she simply didn't want to write one alone.

So this book is a result of joining two hearts—across generations, cultures, immigration, race, and class. Although we are distinct individuals, we are also deeply connected in a community of "We." We have different life experiences, yet have a shared set of lessons from being woven into a broad fabric of community and connection.

When we decided to write this book, we made a commitment that the process itself would be joyful. We found ourselves swimming in a pool of respect, love, and care for one another, which made this book a delight to write, and we hope that our readers will find similar ways to express their leadership within a context of connection and joy.

Collaborating in this way was deeply satisfying and remarkably productive. We found ourselves honing our own wisdoms as we dialogued, laughed, told stories, and then told some more. As you read, you might notice that although our individual voices are sometimes very clear, we chose not to identify which story is whose. This is a deliberate decision based on the fact that though our stories differ, they spring from very similar roots, and we wanted to weave our voices into a choir, rather than only offer solos. We wanted to share specific lessons learned from our unique experiences while decentering particularity, because truly the invitation is to not be alone, isolated, or solo, but instead to trust what emerges in partnership.

Turns out that writing a book, just like leadership, is a non-linear process. We talked, wrote, edited, adjusted, crafted, and rewrote. What we have here is our most heartfelt and honest offering to people committed to creating a world that works for all: leaders working to interrupt old patterns of burnout and martyrdom, and those who want to experiment in new and innovative ways.

Over the years we've learned that leading can often be challenging, that there are times when it's tempting to give up, but we also learned that in the end, it is so very worth it. Good leadership creates possibilities that never existed before: it allows us to create the conditions wherein humans and all life can thrive. We invite you to join us as we explore what it means to lead in these very uncertain times.

Akaya Windwood and Rajasvini Bhansali

An Invitation to Practice Joy in Leadership

We like to visit together in our gardens, surrounded by flowers and cats and fruit trees. We chat and laugh and cry and spill the tea and share our lives and visions for the future.

Each of us swims in a sea of infinite trust. We wrote this book because we believe that human beings can and must transform, both individually and as a species. (We wouldn't have spent more than sixty collective years of experience as executives, trainers, and coaches if we didn't!) But we also wrote this book because we believe that humans are standing on a dangerous precipice in time. As we witness one climate catastrophe after another, we understand the future of the Earth as we know it is imperiled. We are watching as governments and institutions crumble, and it is increasingly clear that old ways of addressing problems are ineffective and often harmful.

Humans face an ever-widening gap of economic inequality, significantly different patterns of global immigration, and what seems like an exponential increase in new viruses and variants. Against this maelstrom of rapid change, the leadership tools of the past are inadequate to address current and future needs. We have hard choices ahead of us, and absent strong, thoughtful, and purposeful leadership, we risk leaving our descendants a depleted world and robbing them of any hope for creating a better one. We owe them more than that.

Joy is an approach to leadership centered in wholeness, celebration, and staying in the work for the long haul. It is a state of mind, a way of being oriented in the heart and in the spirit. You cannot "think" your way to joy: it is a felt, settled state of delight, contentment, confidence, faith, and hope. It isn't located in the ego: it sits next to love and is the yin to the yang of grief. It is an essential part of a human life, a birthright that often is stolen from us during childhood.

Joy is a choice, and we need to keep our eyes out for the moments when choosing joy is possible. Reclaiming joy is transgressive: it allows us to step beyond the limits of rigid socialization and transactional habits, and to lead with clarity of purpose and commitment. Joy is dangerous: it is a threat to systems of control and power-over and is therefore one of the best tools we have as leaders making change. It allows us to move from extracting from others for our self-centered benefit toward transformation for all society.

Why is this important? Because over the years we've seen brilliant and passionate leaders get lost in fatigue, overwork, bitterness, and doing work that is not satisfying. This is such a loss! Systemic oppressions like racism, sexism, classism, ableism, and ageism can suck the spirit from the best of leaders—not to speak of capitalism and its overwrought focus on productivity rather than intrinsic human worth.

Joyless, obligatory, and solely transactional leadership has gotten us into the current fixes we are in, in so many sectors. We need new paradigms that center joy because it expands our human capacity to lead, sustains us even when times are hard, and allows for new ways to enact and receive leadership.

We certainly don't have all the answers, but we know that humanity's future is threatened if it remains in the hands of patriarchal, racist, and colonial institutions built in the nineteenth and twentieth centuries. In this time of increasingly multicultural, multigenerational, and complex organizations and social movements, our intention is to help you chart a path that supports your authentic leadership for the long run. We are convinced that the wisdom of Black and Brown women in principled leadership can offer all of us some universal wisdom.

Leading with Joy is for those who are committed to creating a world that works for all—leaders working to interrupt old patterns of burnout and martyrdom, and those who want to experiment in new and innovative ways. Leading in these turbulent times requires great courage and imagination, and no one person can bring about the kinds of change we need—our world needs millions and millions of inspired, interconnected leaders.

Imagine leadership that is bold, interesting, exciting, and rooted in community and joy. Imagine leaders of organizations and social movements who are rested, ready, and eager. So much would be possible!

Over the years we've learned that leading can often be challenging, that there are times when it's tempting to give up, but we've also learned that in the end, it is so very worth it. Good leadership creates possibilities that never existed before—it allows us to create the conditions wherein humans and all life can thrive. We invite you to join us as we explore what it means to lead in these very uncertain times.

This book is an offering for a young person in a small rural town who knows they want to do something to change their community but doesn't quite know where to start. It is also for a seasoned professional living in a capital city—someone who has been leading people, organizations, or businesses for a long time. And it is for anyone who wants to be a part of creating the conditions for a just and thriving future for the coming generations.

No matter how you identify, we want everyone working toward a world where each human is valued, dignified, and cared for to read this book and know that you are not alone. You are part of a community of devoted souls, alive and gone, who long for transformation and who have committed their lives to it. We have been where you are, curious like you are, confused like you are, tired like you are, dedicated like you are, enchanted like you are. We both come from a long lineage of freedom-seekers, and we have long dreamed about and worked for social change.

In many ways, this book is a journey. It is a series of vignettes about some of our experiences, with reflection questions at the end of each one. Our hope is that the stories each illuminate a particular aspect of leadership and give you an opportunity to reflect on how you lead and what you're learning as you grow as a leader.

These are some of the elements we'll explore:

- Purpose and vision

- Humility, experimentation, and growth

- Preserving and honoring individual and collective dignity

- Healing, forgiveness, and redemption

- Kindness, trust, and compassion

- Grief, challenge, and disappointment

- Keeping the circle whole and healthy

- Flexibility, creativity, and adaptability

- Taking risks and staying steady

- Learning to care for ourselves as we care for our communities

There is no "right" way to read this book (much like there is no "right" way to lead). Some may choose to read for a few minutes a day, absorbing it slowly over time. Others may read it straight through over a weekend. Some may choose to read it out of order— there is no wrong way to read it. We see this book as a conversation between ourselves and you, the reader. No matter how you read it, we want you to know that we believe that everyone can lead, and that each of us inherently has the potential to become an effective and grounded leader.

Leading with Joy is rooted in our intentions, our triumphs, and our mistakes, in our frailties and our strengths. We continue to learn on our leadership journeys, especially in these uncertain times, and trust that you will too. We carry a deep and abiding trust in each reader's intelligence and ability to connect and grow, so start where you are—that's the perfect place to be. We hope this book inspires you to lead with purpose and creativity and to create the conditions for those around you to do their best work...together. If this book helps you remember who you are and why you're doing what you're doing, we will have done a very good thing.

Please come along—let's chart a new course together, uncertainty and all.

CHAPTER 1

Purpose and Vision

Cultivating joy requires commitment and practice. Clarity of both purpose and vision centers us in why we lead and what we want to happen in our work and the world. It is our north star and our place of deepest inspiration. Without it, our leadership can wither and become transactional rather than transformative. Work grounded in purpose and vision is a wonderful source of joy.

Choosing on purpose

At the end of 2020, I was invited to moderate a large event that was going to feature a well-known Black senatorial candidate. My first reaction was, "Oh, ain't I something? I'm gonna moderate a panel with this politico." Then I looked at the date and realized I would have to move certain things around. Nonetheless these political operators were inviting me, and I was feeling myself.

But then I had the second thought, which was, "Why would I want to do that?" No disrespect to the panelists or the organizers who were creating that space, but ultimately, for me, it would have been a performative event that would require my vital time and energy, even if it was strategic and necessary for political debate.

Once I got my little self out of the way and listened, I realized it would take a lot away from my central work and it would be difficult to shift my other commitments. I simply declined, saying, "I'm just not available."

The minute I wrote that to the organizers, I heaved this huge sigh of relief.

The world needs us as leaders to be only and always *on purpose*. And if it's not on purpose, don't do it. I know that I'm on purpose when I get filled up and excited by an idea, not drained. I'm just jazzed to think about it.

As leaders, how much time do we spend *on purpose*? And when we are not, what could that time and energy be used for otherwise?

Reflection 🦋 noitɔɘflɘꓤ

- Where or when has your ego led you to say yes to something that depleted your time and energy?

- Where do you spend your time and energy *not* on purpose?

- How do you gauge whether something is on purpose for you or not?

Thrive where you're planted

Several years ago, I noticed a stick growing in my neighborhood a few doors down from my house. It was right at the edge of the curb, angling out into the street. I didn't pay too much attention to it.

Within a year, I could see it was a fig tree. There were little-bitty figs clinging to the branches. I was sure that someone from the city would come by and cut it down—clearly it was a "volunteer" fig, as no one in their right mind would have planted it so close to the street and at such an angle.

This year it is almost as tall as I am and is filled with the most delicious bright green figs—you can't buy these beauties even in gourmet shops!

I've been quietly rooting for the little tree over the years, hoping that no one would cut it or decide that it was a "nuisance." Each summer I've welcomed the new leaves and fruit, glad that they grace our very urban street. Each summer our tree has brought sweetness to those who pass by (and I've noticed that the fruit isn't wasted—I'm surely not the only one who is harvesting).

There are those who would say that the tree shouldn't be there. It's a hazard to drivers and could make a mess if the fruit should fall. They have a point. Meanwhile I've been rejoicing that it continues to grow and thrive—it's a reminder about deep purpose. All that fig "knows" is that it's here to seek the sun and make sweet fruit. It is not concerned with zoning laws or arboreal civic planning. It is busy doing what trees do, photosynthesizing, sending roots down for water, and sending out oxygen—a gift to humans everywhere. That fig was going to be a fig tree independent of where it was planted. It might not have grown so big or so rapidly, but it was going to be a fig no matter what!

Like fig trees, each of us has a purpose and it doesn't matter where we find ourselves. Our purpose doesn't change. It is crucial as

leaders that we get in touch with and understand why we're here—
what our unique purpose is.

Unlike fig trees, humans can move about the world. We are not
limited to wherever a passing bird might leave its droppings. We
can seek work that allows us to express our purpose fully or choose
organizations that will enable us to thrive. It is our responsibility as
leaders to find the best environments in which to bring and express
our biggest gift—our purpose.

We humans are so lucky to have cousins like the fig to grace our
lives and teach us. My neighborhood is so lucky to have our particular tree, and I am grateful for all the love and support I receive from
my communities.

Reflection

- How clear are you about your purpose—why are you here? Are
  you in the right and best place for you to bring your gift?

- Are the people around you the best people to support your
  purpose?

- Do the structures around you allow you to thrive as a leader?

- Is there anything that needs to shift, begin, or end?

Staying on purpose

There are lots of feelings swirling these days: fear, outrage, outrage about who has the right to be outraged. There are feelings of sadness, grief, helplessness, and being overwhelmed. I'm sure there are many more, and it seems like I've felt them all. Why all the hatred? How come folks are so cruel to each other? In the words of Rodney King, "Can we all get along?"

I don't know.

But I do know that any response I (or a community or a country) may make will rarely be a good one when it comes from a state of anger or fear. I know that my *best* first response under turbulent circumstances is to be still and listen to my heart, to attend to my inner knowing. Otherwise, I will only react and replicate the very thing I'm reacting to—and that generally only leads to more mess.

Moving toward stillness is somewhat counterintuitive when faced with hostility and possible annihilation. However, in that moment of pause it is possible to take a breath and consider options. And there are *always* options—never only a single possibility.

If I wait until my emotional waters are still, I can respond in ways that allow me to bring kindness, creativity, and my best wisdom to whatever situation I'm in. One of the most efficient ways to still my waters is to take a breath and connect to my purpose.

My personal life purpose is to remember that there is no person outside the human circle—every single one of us belongs. There really is no "them" or "us" even when it is politically or emotionally convenient for me to pretend otherwise. I am the eager concert-goer and the young man who strapped bombs onto his precious body. I am the Syrian refugee fleeing tyranny and I am the U.S. legislator demanding we close our borders. Thich Nhat Hanh teaches us this in his poem *Please Call Me by My True Names*. When I remember this, I can consider more clearly what kind of response I choose to make when confronted with complexity and outrage.

I invite you to reflect on your purpose. Why are you here on this planet at this time? What is it that you, uniquely, are here to offer? Give yourself the gift of time to sit with this question awhile.

When you've come to stillness, ask: What is mine to do in this situation?

And when that becomes clear, do that.

I believe that if we all take the time to pause, listen in, and get clear on our purpose, then we have the capacity to respond to a changing and unpredictable world in fresh and creative ways. A legion of purposeful people leading with kindness, compassion, and interconnection is something of great beauty and power. Let us work to make that the case.

Reflection 🦋

- What is your habitual response when you feel overwhelmed or angry?
- Is this how you want to regularly respond as a leader?
- What other options do you have in moments of fear or outrage?

Imagine

> "It is hard for us to imagine what we cannot see."
>
> SALLY RIDE

True, and yet we *must* imagine.

Lately I've been experimenting with centering my time and attention on the world that so many of us are working hard to create. I imagine it tirelessly—it has become almost a prayer. The world right around the corner whose breath Arundhati Roy can hear. I love spending time and energy working toward something we can't yet see, can only imagine, that emerges from wholeness and our deepest heart's desire.

These days I'm listening for transformation, where we move not from vanilla to chocolate, but from vanilla to music! I'm willing to take great leaps of faith—to be foolish, wasteful, and extravagant in my imagination. It's the only way I can see that will get us through and beyond our current moral and political crises.

Why not dare to imagine? It's terrific fun, makes many things possible that weren't otherwise, and vastly increases our appetite for engaging the world. After the past several years of deep imagining, I have to say that I am significantly more resilient, creative, and immensely happier as a result. *This* is a space from which I can authentically and whole-heartedly lead.

Some might say that this is pie-in-the-sky dreaming. Perhaps it is, but it is deeply rooted in and from my Black woman's wisdom born of many years of lived experience. I know in my bones that it is time to turn my attention away from anything that saps our spirits, kills our children, rapes our lands, or robs us of our humanity. I am no longer willing to spend my time attending to a system that never intended for most of us to survive, let alone thrive.

Even those of us who are working deep in the belly of the beast (and I so appreciate those who are) need time to rest, dream, and envision this fast-approaching world. All of us deserve respite from the soul-killing work of living in a toxic and hate-filled political and social arena. Imagining is not mere whistling in the dark—it is a potent act of transformation and world building. It is the process by which we locate our north stars and find our way to liberation.

I invite you to join me out in this fertile field of possibility! We have nothing to lose, everything to gain, and I have a strong notion that our children's children's children will sincerely thank us for it.

Reflection  noitɔɘ⅃ɘЯ

- Get in touch with one of your deepest heart's desires, then spend some time imagining it coming true.
- What might be possible if you led from your heart's imagination?

Power, preparation, and practice

We often get asked by young women, particularly young Black and Brown women, "How do you just walk in the room and act like you own it?" As queer women of color, this question matters because we are up against race, gender, class, caste, and culture—our histories co-influence what happens all the time. While we don't want to be bound by the dysfunction of our histories, they are in the room with us. To know yourself and who you are, and to navigate others' perceptions of you means that Black and Brown women leaders are constantly(!) negotiating power.

To show up in our own power is actually a matter of discipline and strategy.

The first step is doing our homework. Before we walk into any room, we know the answer to these questions: "Who am I trying to move? For what purpose? What's my goal?" It's not just the fierce outfit we wear or what we say. We show up well prepared. We enter with an assessment of who we're trying to organize and for what purpose, and our "why" is clear.

Another important step is to commit to the continuous spiritual practice of affirming our own worthiness and the value of life. We do this so that when we walk into the room, we know it is not an accident. We recognize the leap of faith it takes to be in the room representing the more just and equitable world we are building. We hold deep in ourselves that we belong there, and we practice moving from a place other than ego.

Women are often socialized to take on a lot of responsibility, ignore ourselves completely, and put everyone else first. We're really practiced at false humility. But this can be a way of stepping away from the power that we actually can and do have. In this time, it's vital that Black and Brown women are not tentative about whether there is a role for their leadership.

It is time for people who have traditionally been blocked from leadership to say yes to the full magnitude of power we can exert in the world. We can do this in recognition of Black and Brown women's wisdom as universal wisdom.

Leaders who are young women of color in particular are met with a lot of contempt in doing so: "Who are you? How dare you make decisions for the rest of us?" They are walking the line of trusting their own leadership, while navigating constant criticism and attempts to diminish them.

No matter how prepared—literally or spiritually—we are, we will be dealing with people who find it difficult to reconcile with the power of women of color. Anytime anybody doesn't fit in a box, it's a mirror that forces self-reflection and can be very uncomfortable for others. Thus, we have to again return to our preparation and practice.

Let us constantly learn how to calibrate the use of our own power: how to be both self-assured and confident, and also clear on what's best for everyone.

Reflection  noitɔɘlɟɘЯ

- How do you know your power? Carry your power? Use your power?
- Who are the people in your life who have supported you to recognize and use your own power?
- How are power and freedom related for you?
- What are the ways you prepare and practice to "own the room"?

No longer a pipe dream

I facilitated a meeting of financial leaders and activists focused on creating new economic models in 2020. The group was diverse, international, many genders, ranging in age from early twenties to mid-fifties—all people actively doing this work.

As the meeting started, I noticed that the end of patriarchy and white supremacy kept coming up consistently. I thought, "Okay, y'all name it."

And then they continued to name it and name it and name it as a context for all of their work. The men talked about it. The women talked about it. The people of color. I mean, everybody talked about it, including the four or five white men in the room.

It was a clarity that I have never heard in my life. I was stunned. Of course, they represent a certain cohort of people in the world, but there they were, the words were just coming out of their mouths. It wasn't performative of their wokeness.

I realized that this thing—this end of patriarchy and white supremacy—is no longer a pipe dream. I remember talking about it as a young woman and it's here. It hasn't fallen completely, obviously, as the Trump years revealed. But this moment for me was just a huge indicator of these oppressive systems falling down.

Reflection  noitɔɘ﬚૭Я

- **What spaces do you inhabit where transformative change seems more possible?**
- **What evidence can you see of a change you once thought only possible that is now achievable?**

The near-death experience

My brother says I had my eyes closed and a smile on my face as the van we were in hurtled toward the edge of the cliff. The brakes had failed on a hairpin turn while driving us to a village in rural Meghalaya, miles outside of the city of Shillong in northeast India. The fifteen or so passengers in the van were screaming as bodies slammed about the cabin. The driver, a Bangladeshi refugee, exercised great brilliance in the midst of what promised to be a life-ending crisis and slammed the front of the bus into a hillside. I was sure this was it, and I took to a meditation of gratitude and letting go. It has, after all, been a pretty good life. If this was it, I was all right with it.

This is how I did not die.

The van landed on its left side. All humans and luggage from the right side ricocheted and then landed on those of us on the left side of the van. When I reopened my eyes, a thin older man had fallen on top of me, my own body acting as his shield against the broken windows. Several folks, including my colleague Rajiv and my brother Roveen, had concussions. Adrenalin kicked in and I immediately got to work getting folks out of the bus along with one other person, a firefighter who just happened to be in our van as a vacationer. We dragged injured and confused people out of the van to the side of the road. Then fuel started leaking out of the van and an explosion seemed imminent.

I had felt no fear of death until I looked toward my brother. I imagined having to explain to my two little nephews why their dad didn't make it back from the Indigenous Tierra Madre conference, the largest-ever global gathering of Indigenous people to discuss food and agriculture.

Beyond human calculation, all passengers survived this accident. We ended up in a nearby clinic for a medical checkup and treatment for all those with broken bones. Our lives, however, were undeniably changed.

I look back at that instant when my mind realized the danger and my body calmed the brain. In that brief moment, I went into a meditative stance of surrender. My heart and spirit followed the body, and I was deeply peaceful as I prepared to die. Then the mind followed and prepared to let go. I was one of two from among the fifteen passengers without any injuries. Of course, much of it was luck, but the role of taking an easeful, peaceful stance in times of crises and danger has stayed with me.

The next year, my father was diagnosed with Stage 4 kidney cancer and then multiple myeloma. He fought cancer with all his might and in the end, I was with him as he let go. Had I not nearly died a year prior to this, I might not have been able to show up as his caregiver, grounded in the temporality of life and able to meet each moment with a peaceful heart.

Almost dying was a teacher on how to live fully.

Even now, I do not fear death.

I approach each day as if it's the most important yet, and I end each day feeling complete.

Reflection

- How do you show up in times of crisis and danger?
- How does letting go of fear feature in your leadership?
- Who needs to receive your gratitude right now?

PRACTICE

Discovering our purpose is challenging to do alone. We invite you to chat with a pal or a group of folks you care about, and think back on the moments in your life that brought you joy or deep satisfaction. Tell each other some of the stories of those times.

Do you notice a theme or a thread that connects those moments? Is there an overall story to be told? Try and name it in a simple sentence like "My purpose is to ask hard questions so that people can grow." Or "My purpose is to bring hope wherever I go."

Don't rush with this—our understanding of our purpose deepens over time. As you do this, notice how it feels to talk about joy and purpose.

Imagine the future you want for a great-great-great-great-grandchild or any young one who comes after you. Give yourself the gift of using your deep imagination: Where does this child live? What does "school" look like? Who is in their community? What does the natural world around them look like? Notice how the child moves. What does life feel and look like for this beloved child of your future?

Notice that this child is directly connected to you, even though centuries may separate you. Imagine dedicating your life and work in service to that child and the world around them. How might this inform, impact, or influence your current leadership?

CHAPTER 2

Humility, Experimentation, and Growth

Joy is generated from and lives in the heart, not the ego. We cannot "think" our way to joy. There is no hierarchy of expertise, and no human is better than any other. Remembering that we are only a small and necessary part of a vast human family allows us to do our particular work—to do what is ours and only ours to do—and let others do their particular work. This frees us, because no one of us can possibly do everything that needs doing but together we can accomplish miracles. Being clear about our particular work with purpose and joy is an act of liberation.

We cannot heal what we cannot name

COVID-19 is illuminating the horrific, oppressive, and inequitable underbelly of our U.S. social structures. There is nothing new or fresh in what we are seeing, we are merely witnessing the latest variations of a system initiated at Plymouth Rock in 1620. Since this is a global pandemic, I imagine that this is true all over the world, but I live here in the United States and will only speak from what I know.

We are at a crossroads, and each of us has a choice to make. We can go back to sleep, whistle in the dark, and hope the boogeyman goes away, thereby ensuring that the old roots regenerate. Or we can refuse to cooperate any longer, take action, and create new paths based on principles of fairness, justice, and the interconnection of all life.

Each of us chooses with every breath and action, daily. What will we choose?

I'm committed to a new path, perhaps the harder path, of opening my eyes and heart and refusing to pretend that things were "good back then." I'm committed to keeping my eyes on the stars and my feet on the ground and dancing lightly on the planet as we create new ways of being.

This means I am committed to refusing to turn away from what makes me uncomfortable. I'm committed to sitting with ambiguity and lots of "I don't know," to remembering that I am not well unless all of us are well. This means that I commit to the painfully joyous work of waking up, stretching into new ways of thinking and acting, and reaching for liberation. It's now or never.

The road ahead will be challenging and once we're on it, there is no turning back. We are going to need each other, because there are no individual bootstraps for this journey. We can't go it alone (and we never really could).

We'll need lightweight backpacks and there won't be any maps. We'll need great courage and whining will not help. This journey is not for the faint of heart and will ask much of us.

That said, if we agree to take this journey, we can create new and magnificent ways of being human. We can knit ourselves into the living fabric that surrounds us, understanding that we are a needed but not supreme part of the whole. This will require that we take the risk of falling in love with each other and the rest of the natural world over and over, even when we are weary and want to give up. This is not an easy task, but I believe that it is the only way through.

So come on y'all, let's risk it. Put on your hiking boots or your ballet slippers, pack up your bravery, some snacks to share, and bring a pal or two. I'll meet you on the road.

Reflection

- What is your unique contribution to our collective journey?

- What might you need to learn or change in order to more fully bring your gifts?

- How might you fall in love with and not give up on those who depend on your leadership?

Dance lightly

Tsunamis. Unemployment. Volcanoes. Firestorms. Homelessness.
Ukraine. The Midwest. Pirates. Earthquakes. Drug and human
trafficking. Union busting. Collapsing economies. Dropout rates.
Nuclear fallout. Foreclosures. Floods. Pandemic.

Warm rains. Youth-led movements. Birdsong. Plum blossoms.
Racial justice work in LGBTQ communities. Joy Harjo. Sweet peas.
More than 100,000 people in Madison. Cross-sector collaborations.
Days growing longer. Foal season. Women in Egypt. Late winter full
moons.

It's a busy and fascinating time. Plenty going on to capture our
attention.

As leaders, it can sometimes feel that it is our responsibility to
respond to *everything*. I've been watching people valiantly try to find
some way to do something about all that's going on. The world can
seem quite overwhelming right now.

Truth is, each of us can only do what each of us can do. I have
to trust that someone else is tending to the things I cannot. And I
must continue to do my part, because someone else is counting on
me. No one of us can possibly respond to everything. We need each
other and partnership is essential.

While I'm very aware of what those close to me are up to, I also
have to trust in the efforts of people I may never encounter. I am
clear that my fate is inextricably linked to the work of some young
woman in Cairo whose name I will never know. We are mutually
accountable, even if we never meet.

What does it mean to be in partnership with unknown kin? What
is my relationship to the woman in Cairo? What might be my cove-
nant with her?

As I think about it, good partnership requires attention to personal well-being and sustainability. It does not serve the woman in
Cairo for me to be worried sleepless or to neglect my welfare. It does

her absolutely no good when I eat on the run rather than take the time to be grateful for what sustains me. And I want the same for her. I sincerely hope that she has time to restore herself—that she gets enough rest and that she pauses to hug the children around her.

Personal sustainability requires balance. And it requires deep partnerships and trust. It's important that we pay as much attention to the natural rhythms of the earth and the wonderful things going on in our lives, as we do to all of our challenges. And as effective long-term leaders, it's important to remember that we don't need to take care of all of the challenges in the world. It is necessary to trust and support our kin where they may best lead. We live in wonderful, terrible times. Both in equal measure.

Negotiating both the gifts and challenges of these times requires us to move forward as agents of change by doing the best work we can do in the places we can be most effective. And at the same time to dance lightly, in our lives and on the planet. So I invite you to dance—lightly and in partnership. Let's remember that we're not alone, that we can solve what needs solving because we're all connected. You, me, and the young woman in Cairo.

Reflection

- Who are you counting on?
- Who needs to be able to count on you?
- Imagine your connections to those you don't yet know...

"I don't know"

One day, I realized that I didn't have to have all the answers. Whew, was that a day of deep liberation!

In the early days of running a national organization, I was always trying to figure out how to make everything go. Years prior, I'd been a disastrous executive director and had vowed never to do that again. Twenty years later there I was, leading another organization. I found myself saying to myself over and over, "I don't know how to do this. I just don't know how to do this."

Around that time, a spiritual mentor said to me, "Consider 'I don't know' as a significant and strong place in the universe." When we think we know something so well (or better than others), we often limit our own growth possibilities because we jump ahead to define and explain something before we fully understand it.

From this I learned that when I had the courage to say "I just don't know," I was essentially telling myself that all things are possible.

My mentor continued, "It's actually a powerful stance to *not* know."

That conversation really made me sit up and realize that if *knowing* limits my possibilities, then it's wise to spend a good portion of my time as a leader in reflection and rest. This allows me to *know* from a deeper place, which makes my decisions much more grounded and trustworthy.

Whether I contemplate this "unknowing" in my meditation, sitting at my altar, or sometimes even in a dream, I find that if I sit in the unknown long enough, some stronger knowing eventually comes. Wisdom arrives, lands, and says, "Here it is." And then I can say "Okay, there it is." I know that those profound moments of clarity occur only because I've actually slowed down enough to hear the wisdom.

After reflecting upon the wise words of my mentor, I stopped trying to be an expert in anything. It grounded my leadership in the fact that there are people who know far more than I do about many things. It changed how I hired people—I started looking for those who knew much more about their areas of expertise than I could ever know. Why should we, as leaders, compete with those with better knowledge or experience? This freed me up to do what I'm here to do, which is to ask "Who's best at X? And how can I support them?" Because I want them to be part of this effort I am trying to build and support.

Leaders need people to remind us that we don't have to, nor should we, have all the answers. Let's remember: many heads are wiser than one alone.

With that in mind, I encourage all of us as leaders to look for the people who will help us to build our visions and movements. Remember: it's liberating that we don't always need to *know*.

Reflection

- Under what conditions is it safe for you to admit that you "just don't know"?

- How do you relate to uncertainty or ambiguity in your leadership?

- How do you slow down enough to listen for your inner knowing to come through?

Authenticity

In 2011, I decided to stop dyeing my hair. I am now officially a gray-haired woman. When I turned fifty-five that year, I made an even deeper commitment to authenticity, and that included looking in the actual mirror (and not just the mirror of expectations the world holds up for women of a "certain age").

I have to say that it's been a bit of a ride. There were many external shifts. I no longer get looked at in "that way" on the street. I've had younger folks give me a seat on public transit. I'm taken seriously in ways I hadn't anticipated. Two months before cutting my locks, I was carded while buying a bottle of wine. Two days after cutting them, I was offered a senior discount.

There have been many internal shifts as well. I now feel free to claim all children as my grandkids and talk to every baby and young person I meet (sometimes to the chagrin of my sweetie, Kim). While I may think twice before making a decision, I've stopped second-guessing myself, and have confidence that my decisions are well considered. Paradoxically, I'm much more willing to be "wrong" and to be influenced by those around me.

Now, I don't want to give the impression that cutting off one's hair and letting it gray is the only path to authenticity. I do, however, highly recommend it for those who are able. At the time, it felt like taking a big risk, but the rewards have been great. I don't give a rat's patootie if someone thinks I'm silly, and as a result I've begun to play a lot more. Literally.

And leading has become a lot more fun and satisfying. I'm finding that my leadership has improved because I'm much less concerned with my image (self or otherwise) and therefore am more flexible.

As I've said many times before, we cannot do anything alone. If we're going to risk being deeply authentic, we need to be in partnership, and that means we'll need to know about each other. To that end, I want to invite you to tell those around you when you've done something terrific—don't hide behind false modesty. If you don't feel comfortable tooting your own authentic horn, toot the horn for some other amazing leaders!

So cut your hair, go back to school, end a toxic relationship, skinny dip, paint your car bright purple— I don't care. Take a risk. I figure the world cannot have too many bold, creative, fun, joy-filled authentic leaders. Let's all sign up for that.

Reflection

- What would be your next big and bold step toward authenticity? Not just a baby step, but an in-your-face, Grandmother type of step?

- What might you gain if you were to take that step—personally and in your leadership? What joy is possible in authenticity?

- What fears come up as you consider this?

The unintentional tree

As my father was dying, I moved him and my mother into our new home together in 2017. I had just bought the house—my first—and the backyard, though generous in size and potential, was barren.

As my father watched and did the work of detaching from this life and preparing for the next, my mother did so much work designing and planting and transforming the space into a thriving garden.

While he was sitting in the backyard one day, Dad ate his very first California nectarine. He'd never had one before.

And as he would have done in India, he just threw the nectarine pit onto the ground. He liked to sit in an armchair in the garden and just throw seeds and peels and pits on the ground when he was done eating them. Some things I would pick up and put in the compost, and some things my mom would actually bury in the ground.

But no one paid attention to this particular pit that day, and now it has grown into a full-fledged nectarine tree.

For a long while we didn't know what kind of tree it was, and because it hadn't started bearing fruit yet, we didn't know what to expect.

Eventually, we learned that this tree was the result of my father's discarded nectarine pit. We also learned it would take three years to fully fruit. It gave us its first bumper crop about six months ago, and it then went completely dormant. Again, we were wondering what this tree would do next.

A few months later, the tree sprouted again. Its pink flowers, the result of my father's careless toss, were beautiful.

And just around his birthday in early summer, the flowers gave way to an abundance of fruit, enough to feed half our block and all our family and friends. And as I write this, my mother is making chutney with a bounty of nectarines, every jar she fills a thanksgiving.

Reflection 🦋

- Where do you look for evidence of change, growth, or shifting energy?

- What wisdom does nature offer you?

- What seeds are you planting, intentionally or inadvertently?

From "I" to "we"

Nobody who does movement work in a disciplined way says, "This is all about me. I made this happen."

A movement orientation to leadership requires us as individual leaders to choose over and over again to separate our "I" from the "we." Movement work changes the culture—a massive feat that is impossible to imagine, let alone accomplish, alone.

Leaders showing up with a "check me out" attitude, showing off their credentials like flashy cars or clothes, are antithetical to a movement orientation to leadership. In social enterprise spaces, we see a lot of "I am the entrepreneur"; "I transformed this organization"; "Look at me, I'm the owner and proprietor."

In movement spaces, it's harder for leaders to get away with that. Movements, by their very definition, are organized groups of people with a shared vision and principled collective action. The discipline it takes to have a shared vision and build a strategy and action plan together means that as leaders we must constantly make decisions that are best for all involved.

Try to identify a decision you have made as a leader that impacted only you. It's not possible! You want to go on a retreat for a week and do some writing? It has an impact on your partner or family, your co-workers, on everyone and everything you are tending to. Leaders have to weigh their own "I" impulses in the context of other beings, otherwise we may as well be tyrants. If we do not recognize how we have been shaped by toxic hyper-individualism, then a reality-TV star becomes the President of the United States, with zero congruence or integrity between his inner and outer life.

Movement leaders are required to show up for everyone, not just their personal aggrandizement. When our movements have been successful, it's because leaders have a very honest assessment of themselves, have integrity within their role, and contribute to the whole.

"I" leaders are often trying to earn their cachet by having the most righteous positions. "We" leaders do not continually center themselves, but are busy putting the work before the persona.

If we are leaders, we must lead *everybody*. As leaders, our central operating question is "What's best for all concerned?"

Yes, "all concerned" includes each of us. And as humans, we are fundamentally in relation to others. In actuality, it is "we" all the time.

Reflection  noitɔɘℓⱭɘЯ

- When can you get lost in your own story about how marvelous you are, or the stories others tell about you? What keeps your ego in check?

- Why do you think narratives of singular, "heroic" leaders exist? How can you subvert them in your work?

- What are you in service *of* (rather than in service *to*) as you gain power as a leader? To whom are you accountable?

Youthful clarity

Young people's shine is in their fervent belief that everything is possible. In their willingness to bring their whole self.

When we envision the future, young people's leadership is what will bring the change.

Young people around the world are super clear that the climate catastrophe is their core issue. Our previous generations worried that our siloed issues would be sacrificed if we pushed for climate justice. Young people see this consistently and intersectionally.

They are bringing their voices to the table and taking many risks, while working more successfully outside of the traditional organizational structure. They don't care about the "big green" funders. They're irrelevant.

The level of coordination on a global scale is breathtaking, and the young people are inventing and originating creative ways of organizing that we have not even thought about. I mean, K-Pop fans and TikTok users foiling a dog-whistle rally for the sitting U.S. President?! When a platform for putting cute dances out in the world becomes a huge political organizing tool, we know we have more to learn.

We "old timers" have a huge learning curve around technology, and the young people are going to show us ways of mass organizing and operationalizing collective action we haven't even begun to scratch.

We have no idea what it is, we can only sense it as a tide coming in. It's not our tide. We're part of the tide that is going out, but young people are where we can always revive our faith.

Reflection

- How do you exhibit faith in young people's leadership? Judgment?

- When do you recognize that young people see possibilities veiled to people with more "experience"?

- How do you attend to the development, protection, and encouragement of the next generations?

Welcome the honesty

Sometimes as strong leaders, we are challenged by the feedback we receive. And it's easy to become indignant! But with our own inner strength, we can also choose to be grateful when someone looks at us and says, "Really!?" or "What'd ya mean?" or "That didn't smell right."

Attending to our own inner strength and wisdom allows us to ask more questions. We can learn, reflect, and make adjustments if need be.

We can be invited to heal what we didn't know was impacting others. We can see where we are hiding from wounded parts of ourselves.

Many of us have been taught to think that feedback is a bad thing and should be avoided. In a society that heralds achievement over failure and stability over change, it's tempting to engage in confirmation bias and validation-seeking behaviors. The last thing we want to hear from people we respect or after getting so much done is, "You don't have it all together as much as you may think you do."

But by welcoming thoughtful (or even challenging) feedback, we can learn from a mirror held up to us, allowing ourselves to go deeper without self-judgment. And with deep self-kindness and an open heart and mind, we can allow ourselves to grow. Often what we've learned from our own family, community, and cultural upbringing is to shut down or fight back against the critic. To shrink in the face of criticism, however, is to fall into the trap of taking down our own leadership. When we avoid feedback, we cannot grow.

So what if we let others' judgments or criticisms have the opposite impact on us? What if we viewed people's feedback as an expression of how much they loved us or something they really cared about?

When beloved people we respect and admire offer feedback, we have the option of receiving it as an affirmation of how deeply they are committed to our not being half-assed—that they respect us enough to tell us about ourselves. Only in a container of love and care is that possible.

And we can remember that any feedback, whether harsh or compassionate, is a needed part of grounded leadership, a part in which we don't have to view ourselves or anyone else with an assumption of fragility. If we can embrace the internal practice of remaining open and pliable and honest with ourselves, rather than constantly trying to cultivate a persona or protect our egos, then feedback doesn't have to come as an assault, or even a surprise.

It can come as a gift.

Reflection

- How can you find joy in feedback?
- How can you build your skills to welcome and accept corrective feedback?
- How can you give joyful feedback?

PRACTICE

Take out a piece of paper and make two lists:

My greatest strengths
as a leader

My greatest learning
challenges—how I need
to grow

Be honest here: no false modesty, please, and no
exaggerations either. Each of us has strengths and
challenges, and it is crucial as leaders that we recognize
both.

Choose one thing from each list. Pay attention to your
strength—honor what you've accomplished and learned.
Notice how you want to grow. Please choose only one
thing; you can't change everything all at once—that would
be impossible, and there is no joy in that.

What is one small, do-able step you will take next week to
strengthen your leadership?

CHAPTER 3

Preserving and Honoring Individual and Collective Dignity

Joy comes from preserving and honoring the dignity of all whom we encounter in our leadership journey. Often, we operate from a place of prioritizing tasks and accomplishments over relationships. This, however, does not lead to transformation. When we uphold the dignity and agency of the people we are trying to lead, influence, or organize, our impact can be so much greater and last long beyond our time in leadership. The vignettes in this section highlight the many ways in which we find joy in dignifying and lifting others, just as we do for ourselves.

Binaries

I've just about had it with the vitriol and saber-rattling lately. Our world cannot sustain much more bellowing from those on one end of a spectrum at those on the other, with no room for nuance, ambiguity, or the unknown. Enough!

Much of our current day "discourse" is framed (at least in the mainstream media) by discussions of who is right/wrong, right/left, bad/good, holy/evil. As long as we are limited to these extremes, we will be doomed to the tyranny of righteousness and posturing. This will not, and cannot, sustain us. There is no joy in this.

Lately, I've had the pleasure of listening to old speeches by Dr. Martin Luther King Jr. His ability to engage ideas and hearts without spewing hatred often moves me to tears. I've so enjoyed hearing (again) his deep and resonant call to accountability and conscience. Somehow, with his commitment and clarity, and without name-calling or viciousness, he managed to move mountains. He didn't get distracted by hatred or vilification. He built, instead, a "Beloved Community."

Sometimes it is so tempting, so very easy to fall into the old comfortable dance of "we the anointed, they the oppressor" or "we the good guys, they the bad." Isn't it oddly enjoyable now and then to assign blame and condemn those with whom we disagree? I do it more often than I care to admit. Delicious. And dangerous.

And then I come to my senses and take the more difficult road of really trying to listen to those with whom I vehemently disagree. This means I must set aside my notions of who I think they are and who I think I am. I have to be willing to be changed by what I hear. This is terribly challenging sometimes, but I find that when I'm willing to stop and really listen—with my heart as well as with my ears—I learn something. I grow. I change.

Biologists tell us that the most interesting, diverse, and evolving places are at the edges of ecosystems, where unlike organisms come into contact with one another. And science is showing us that cooperation—not competition—is actually the best means of collective survival. What if we humans began to act as though we were part of the ecosystem and were to sidle up to and explore difference rather than fear or annihilate it?

Many are working hard toward creating a world where leaders, both those in the halls of Congress and those in kindergarten, can gather freely and exchange ideas. Such leaders are dreaming of a world where killing and torture are unthinkable, where we can disagree without mayhem.

This is a call to hearts. Let us interrupt the tendency to sort into "either/or," to look for opportunities to blame, or to create enemies. Let's explore some edges and find new ways to dance.

Good leadership depends on our willingness to engage new and perhaps uncomfortable ideas. It depends on our willingness to be changed by what we encounter, and to grow. In fact, the world depends on it.

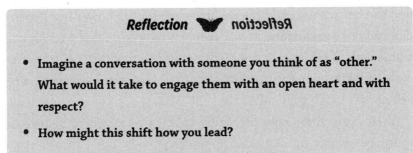

Reflection

- Imagine a conversation with someone you think of as "other." What would it take to engage them with an open heart and with respect?
- How might this shift how you lead?
- What might be possible for you? For them?

Pluralism as practice

Cultural knowledge is essential fuel for transformation. In my case, Jain beliefs have been so deeply embedded in my consciousness that unpacking their influence on my daily acts needed some deliberate reflection. I was raised as a Jain, which for me means that I learned lessons on how to live from my grandparents and parents. These were not dogmatic lessons but instead subtle lessons that imbued all interactions. Jainism, as I understand it, is a philosophy that encourages reflective individual ethical and spiritual conduct. Only then is collective liberation possible. The consequences of our choices are not pre-ordained by some higher power but dependent on our own actions. It is a deeply intersectional and ecological framework of ethics, not rules. Ultimately, to free the soul from the cycle of birth and rebirth toward liberation requires a discipline of self as part of a bigger collective.

There were three core principles that I was raised to believe in that have greatly influenced my practice.

- **Ahimsa** or nonviolence: This invitation is to radically minimize one's impact on all living beings. Life imbues even the tiniest of microorganisms and every life form is inviolably sacred and worthy of reverence. All life forms and sentient beings have the innate, irrevocable right to live and blossom. So to cultivate this right to life, for our own selves, we choose to practice nonviolence not only with our bodily movements, inner thoughts, and speech but also diet, vocation, and habitual patterns. In my life, this means holding a gentleness of spirit in how I work and live—toward my colleagues, collaborators, and comrades and also toward myself. This means to tend to my health and well-being, knowing that my body and spirit are sacred and to also create conditions for my team and all those who work with us to experience wellness.

- **Anekantavada** or multiplicity of viewpoints: This invitation
  is to resist all forms of philosophical and ideological dogma,
  supremacy of any form in ideas, actions, or thoughts. This
  worldview encourages collaboration across deep differences,
  pettiness, ego, and competitiveness. It reminds us that
  uncertainty is a core virtue, that change is inevitable and feels
  so critical for leading in these times, through the dynamics
  of the pandemic, uprisings, and human discontents. We have
  to give up our fixations and be willing to learn from constant
  experimentation and mistakes. In my life, this means that
  as righteous as I might feel in my politicized beliefs, I have
  to be willing to deeply listen to others' views. The regime of
  truth that we perpetuate as leaders constricts innovation and
  creativity. Anytime I notice that I have begun to hold certain
  viewpoints as absolute, I turn to my colleagues to inquire if
  there are wisdoms I am ignoring! And every single time, I
  am reminded that my best decisions are those that take into
  account a multiplicity of viewpoints. This is not to give way
  to indecisiveness but simply to remember that my absolutist
  tendencies do not serve the best of the whole.

- **Aparigraha** or non-accumulation/non-hoarding: This is
  an invitation to live simply so others may simply live. It is
  human to have feelings of possessiveness that cause greed
  and selfishness to arise: this is mine, I did this. The practice
  of aparigraha at a collective level holds the promise to free us
  from resource extraction, deforestation, fossil fuel addiction,
  and labor exploitation. It moves us toward discipline,
  simplicity, abundance, and equanimity in our daily lives.
  In my life, this means that as I support others in resource
  redistribution and reparations, I too must look at the ways
  in which I give in to hoarding—of emotions, of spirit, of

love, of stuff. It is an invitation to give more abundantly and generously without expectation or return.

noitɔɘꙆꙷɘꙄ

Reflection

- What do these principles evoke for you?
- Which of these principles comes naturally to your leadership?
- Which one of these is a challenge?
- What support do you need to practice?

Lifelines and open doors

I stood before the room of strangers, nervous and shaky, naming my audacious vision:

"We will be the gold standard of how the Global North and the South relate to each other."

At the beginning of every Rockwood Leadership Institute program, each participant is given a simple task: stand in front of the group, speak for two minutes about the future you plan to create as a leader, and, at the end, calmly and confidently accept the resulting applause without looking away, squirming, or deflecting with humor.

The room was pretty unresponsive. Because most of the people in the room were U.S.-based folks, it seemed no one gave a damn about what I was saying about internationalism. At the time I ran an organization with a $200,000 deficit and a half-million-dollar budget, and so I started to think, "Who am I with all of these big aspirations?"

And then I saw this sweet face just beaming at me from the back of the room. This face, Akaya's, said to me at that moment, "You can be anything you want to be. I believe in you."

When I think back, this was one of the hardest periods in my career, but seeing and feeling and soaking in that authentic beam of light gave me the courage to get up the next day and deal with the white donors who didn't want to talk to me.

We can't lose sight of the fact that such extension of care and upholding of possibility, especially for women of color in this moment in the world, is actually a lifeline.

When the world is harsh and unkind, that one human who shows you that they believe in you makes all the difference.

When Rajasvini stood there and talked about what she was going to do, I knew that I trusted her vision and I was going to accompany her in its manifestation. I remember thinking at the time, "Oh, I see you. I see that you need to be here, and that you have the potential to be hugely influential in philanthropy."

It's important for me to invite people, particularly young Black and Brown women, to step into positions of leadership that they would never have even seen for themselves, to offer them legitimacy in their journey. If a person has the courage to walk through that door, I can and will hold it open. I have no interest in being a gatekeeper.

Now, what that person does with it once they go through the door is up to them. There have been a few times when I've lifted people into positions of leadership and influence that they were not ready for, and things did not turn out as I'd hoped.

That said, do I regret my choices? Would I have it any other way? No.

Opening doors is what we need to do for one another. A person may soar and they may fail. They may be mediocre. I can't control any of that. Even if what I see and who a person is aren't quite the same, I am always going to try to bring folks along. Even if I am disappointed sometimes, I refuse to let go of my commitment of trying to see the best in people. Sometimes I can see something in someone that they can't yet see in themselves. And as leaders, that's an important part of our job.

Reflection

- Who has believed in you when you felt overwhelmed or doubtful?

- How do you open doors for others?

- When it comes to having faith and trust in people, who do you want to be in your soul and your consciousness?

Seeing the unseen

A colleague and I were walking along the crowded waterfront in San Francisco and coming toward us was a trio of young African American men who were joking and playing. As we crossed paths, I greeted them, and just as the last of them walked by I heard him speak.

"Thanks for seeing us."

It took a minute for that to register.

My companion said, "Did you hear what I heard?"

It took me a moment before I could respond with yes.

My heart was breaking. How could it be that I would be thanked for merely seeing someone? It took all of my self-control not to run back to those young men, gather them in my arms, and apologize for every person who had ever overlooked them, averted their eyes, or turned away.

What must it be like to move through a world that refuses to meet one's eyes, that refuses to acknowledge one's very existence? I could make an analysis and write this piece solely about the kind of pervasive racism that creates a very specific and limiting box in which African American men and boys are expected to live (and why they might feel invisible).

Yet as I scan the world with those young men still in my heart, I notice that many kinds of people are often overlooked. The bag clerk at the grocery market, the person at the front desk, the folks who carry our mail or clean our streets or who are considered too old or too young or too...

What could happen if every day we were to greet each human as though they were worthy of notice and respect? What could happen if every day you were greeted as though you were worthy of notice and respect? What could change?

There is a certain cult of personality even among those of us whose lives are committed to social transformation. A lot of jockeying goes on around who gets noticed for acclaim, who gets the big dollars, who gets the media attention. Many of our organizations are less effective than they could be because of this competition for limelight or resources.

The reality is that most folks working to bring change do so because they care about their community or issue, not because they are looking for recognition or awards. Nonetheless, their work is crucial and necessary and is deserving of respect even if it goes unheralded. They may be unsung, but they are certainly heroes.

I've said for years that everyone takes leadership in some way every day. Everyone. Most acts of leadership go unnoticed or unacknowledged, and that's a shame. The cultural pattern of noticing only some types of leadership and ignoring others contributes to the erasure of large groups of folks—women, poor and working-class people, and, yes, young African American men.

If we can find ways to see each other, to honor the existence of every being who coinhabits this wonderful earth with us, if no young person ever has need to thank a stranger for merely seeing them, then we will have done a fine thing.

Here's my invitation to you: let's take a month and intentionally notice those we would normally not see. Let's interrupt old patterns of not looking into the eyes of "those people" (whoever they are to you). Let's greet and acknowledge the folks we generally walk by or around and watch what happens. Let's say "Hey" to someone new tomorrow. I'll bet we have conversations that surprise us. I'll bet we learn something new.

> ### Reflection 🦋
>
> - What might happen if you greeted or caught the eye of everyone you encountered for a week, especially those you tend to avoid or shy away from?
>
> - What could change in your leadership if those around you saw and consistently acknowledged your worth?
>
> - What could change if you consistently acknowledged the inherent worth of those around you?

Worthy of being alive

The first time I traveled to the African continent, I got off the plane in Nairobi and the taxi driver took me to where I would be staying. As he departed, he said, "Welcome home, sister."

It was all I could do to not burst into tears.

After about a week of that feeling, I realized why I was so emotional on the trip, "Oh, I'm not 'different' here."

In Kenya, women walk in their bodies with particular confidence, with an ease that is unfamiliar to me. Not every woman, certainly, but enough that I noticed it. As I watched women walk, I observed that they didn't carry themselves as "other." They knew something I didn't about the experience of belonging. I realized that in the United States, Black women are never free from the subterranean pressure of simply trying to live.

Ever since, I've been thinking about African-descended peoples living for generations in the United States and places around the world where we are not indigenous. I've been thinking about what it means to be a people who essentially are never at home.

I would ask those of you who are leaders of color whose people moved (forced or otherwise) to imagine a world where you live and lead with ease in your body, knowing you belong. Imagine living and leading without anxiety, without fear. Remember: this is entirely possible. And to those of you who are white allies, I'd ask you to consider how it may feel for those of us who move through the world with trepidation—every day. Without defense, without guilt… please, just imagine, and be aware.

Reflection 🦋 noitɔɘlʃɘЯ

- How do you relate to "the pressure to be alive"?
- What did you learn about belonging in your family of origin/ancestry? Or from/with others who have influenced you?
- Where is home? Who is home? How do you know?

Pandemic and the next Now

I hurtled into 2022 as an optimist. The pandemic is over, I thought. I can travel to see my friends, share a meal, hug them tight again. We can meet as a staff team and have those hallway and happy hour conversations that help transform unnecessary tensions from years of virtual work into positive regard for our teammates. We can build our new strategic plan! I can help handle a lot of my parents' affairs in India. And then I realized that in this third year of a pandemic, it is hard to hold on to optimism, let alone to keep moving at the pace of change once set into motion in a different time and era.

On each work day during the first week of January 2022, someone wept on a video meeting or phone call, sometimes myself! People canceled calls because their children were home sick with Omicron or they had a beloved family member in the hospital. We forgot important appointments. We got really hardened when we heard criticism in a colleague's voice. We got short with each other for no apparent reason.

It was then that I realized that this is a terrifying moment of uncertainty and we humans are tender.

The pandemic right from its start, in Arundhati Roy's wise words, presented an opportunity "to break with the past and imagine [our] world anew. This one is no different. It is a portal, a gateway between one world and the next."

Yet three years later, we are rushing back to what we thought was normal. Instead, perhaps we need to give more time to examine our humanity, to notice our habitual pacing, to understand the depth of our interconnectedness, to attend to our tragedies, so our unprocessed grief, our unmetabolized pain no longer creates messes!

Here's what my team and I reflected on together this January to help us pause, reckon, "imagine anew," and begin to build the next Now:

1. What's a practice that nourishes ourselves that can help us nourish each other?

2. What wins from 2020–2021 should we celebrate?

3. What challenges did we face?

4. What pivots did we make?

5. What lessons did we learn?

6. Based on what you heard, what are one or two moves we will make to mitigate the challenges; further enhance the wins; support the pivots; be wise and grounded in the realities of the current moment for our movements, members, and staff?

7. Based on these reflections, how will we approach/modify/ strengthen our work in 2022 toward our theory of change? How will we adapt our pacing to sustain ourselves and veer toward joy?

Reflection 🦋 ~~Reflection~~

- **What are your reflections on the questions above?**
- **What about your team?**
- **How will you together veer toward sustainability and joy?**

PRACTICE

Close your eyes, take a deep breath, and remember the first time you felt worthy. For some, this moment may be the first time you've thought about it. The truth is that you are, and every human is. Notice what's true for you.

Notice what happens in your body as you contemplate the fundamental truth of your worthiness. This has been true from the moment of your birth. Imagine what might be possible if you never questioned it again.

Close your eyes, take a deep breath, and notice that everyone around you is worthy, and no one is more or less so than anyone else. Notice what happens in your body as you contemplate that fundamental truth.

Imagine what might change in your leadership if you remembered and led from that truth every day.

CHAPTER 4

Healing, Forgiveness, and Redemption

There is much to be enraged by these days. When we as leaders hold on to unhealed wounds, we can inflict harm on the people we seek to lead. Committing to our own healing then becomes critical for creating the conditions in which all can thrive. It is a leadership imperative to continuously work on making ourselves whole. We can find much joy in forgiveness and redemption, not only because they are right, but also because without them, the conditions for joyful exploration, collaboration, and experimentation simply cannot be created. Forgiveness releases us from the bonds of past trauma and creates room for us to be more fully human. It allows us to lay down old histories and lay new spacious and liberating foundations. Forgiveness can be quite challenging, but it is a crucial step on the path toward joy.

Leading from love: The attentiveness that brought accountability

It had been six months since I started my new role as a management advisor for a network of youth polytechnics, or vocational schools, in rural Kenya. The Wakamba village elders in Maseki village where

I lived had named me Mutanu, meaning "one who smiles a lot." My career, coursework, and training in management consulting, policy analysis, community organizing, and organizational development had prepared me well for the task.

Or so I thought.

Within the first few weeks, it was apparent that one of the youth polytechnics had some serious management challenges. While all the polytechnics in the district were resource strapped, with underpaid teachers and impoverished students, at least the others had great leadership and community buy-in. I saw it in parents' willingness to sell a parcel of land to pay for their children's education.

But this one (we'll call it "KYP") never seemed to retain any equipment or students or teachers. Each month, we heard of a new burglary and little by little, all the assets of the institution were disappearing. In the meantime, the principal of the polytechnic appeared to be getting richer. He had built a home for himself—lavish by local standards—and was able to send his children away for higher education, while the polytechnic he ran struggled to survive. It did not take long for me to come to the conclusion that he was embezzling funds, and possibly even organizing these burglaries. The murmurs about his character at the local market only seemed to confirm my suspicions.

I shared my concerns with the coordinating committee of the district's network of polytechnics. Mr. M, a local teacher and community leader, was my direct supervisor in my "capacity building" role. Time after time, I would bring up my animated allegations about how criminal and unethical the KYP principal's behavior was. And each time, Mr. M would patiently nod, listen to all my rants, and then say, "We shall address."

Another week or two would go by, nothing would change, and I would get more and more frustrated. To me, there was no time to waste in seeing the principal of KYP fired and a new principal found.

I had convinced myself that I couldn't be effective in working with the network of polytechnics unless we had the right people in place. Despite all I knew about cultural competence, I found myself falling prey to that often-circulated notion that people in the Global South, particularly in Africa, are conflict averse and slow or reluctant to handle corruption issues.

After a few months of my fruitless ranting and what I deemed inaction, Mr. M finally called a meeting of community leaders at the struggling KYP. The principal under investigation was also present. After the first hour of pleasantries, tea, small talk, and general discussion about the community, I felt myself becoming impatient. In my head, I continued to worry about their lack of confrontation with this man, who so clearly deserved to be brought to justice. But at least I had learned something in my first six months in Kenya— sometimes my most important role was observer.

As the conversation continued well into the second hour, I noticed that Mr. M was skillfully and patiently changing the course of the conversation. He spoke slowly and confidently, sharing that the community had a problem: the inability of one of our institutions to do justice to our children's education. He spoke without any air of malice or judgment of the principal. This collective ownership of what appeared to be one man's and one polytechnic's problem helped me take a deep pause with my internal narrative. What transpired in the room after this shift in the conversation transformed how I have thought about and worked on organizational and leadership development ever since.

The elders sat in silence and invited the principal to reflect on his part in the community's troubles. Mr. M posed gentle yet sobering questions in the spirit of reflection, subtly and powerfully appealing to the principal's sense of shared responsibility to address the polytechnic's ongoing struggles. Initially, the principal got defensive, even angry, but Mr. M continued with his questions. Each one carried the principal to a new level of awareness. Each word offered by the elders demonstrated to the principal the implications of his action for the whole community.

This process of reflection, silence, then call to the collective good continued for another few hours. The principal's anger turned into reflection and then tears. In his breakdown, he not only owned up to embezzlement, but also to having let down his own family, his community, his people, and the generations to come. As the fifth hour of our meeting drew to a close, the principal had made a pledge to return the funds, apologize in public, and to move on and make space for a new leader.

After the meeting, I was in awe of what Mr. M and the committee members had done. Had they approached the principal with derision and singled him out and punished him as I would initially have liked to see, he perhaps would have just gone on to create the same mess elsewhere. But Mr. M and the elders were not guided by their anger. Had they been, they would have denied the principal an opportunity for healing and for redemption. Instead, they choose to preserve the sense of collective responsibility that bound them as a network and as a committee, while offering the principal an opportunity to preserve his personal dignity. I learned that criminalizing is short term and less effective than the process of lasting community accountability.

I am fortunate to have become engaged with an approach to international social-change philanthropy and development that builds the power of grassroots groups and their local leaders. Looking back to my time in Kenya, I now know I was learning what it means to be a self-aware development worker, to listen deeply, to not intervene prematurely, to have deep respect for the process of change and empowerment, to resist the temptation to be an expert, and instead to accompany the process of self-determination and community healing.

Often when I look in the mirror and get real with myself about how I'm behaving as a leader, I remember Mr. M's kind and patient face—ready to listen first, build unity, and then act with compassion. And then I remember I still have a long way to go.

Reflection

- How did the pace and steadiness of Mr. M's approach impact the outcome of the meeting?
- Have you ever been quick to condemn someone after wrongdoing? If so, was the person's capacity for accountability strengthened or diminished as a result?

Join in the wailing

I gave my staff ten days of collective bereavement leave in 2020, because of the pandemic and the many millions of people we have lost. How can we not feel that? My staff were invited to grieve recent and old losses with their communities, families, or by themselves as they wished. As a group of colleagues, we were observing a pause from business as usual, and everybody came back in better shape to carry on.

One of the ancestors that inspired this is Prudence Nobantu Mabele, who was one of our South African comrades when I worked at Thousand Currents. Nobantu was one of the first African women to publicly share her HIV status in South Africa in 1992. At the time, she was confronting head-on the immense shame and stigma that fueled a raging epidemic that would go on to kill fifteen million people on the African continent. She was the founder and director of Positive Women's Network and the founding member of many more organizations addressing HIV, gender-based violence, and LGBTQ rights in South Africa and the rest of the African continent, including the Treatment Action Campaign.

The very first time I met Nobantu, she took me to the countryside to meet a group of indigenous healers in Kwazulu Natal. Now, Prudence never gave you full information or spoke in complete linear sentences. You just had to trust her magic. She put me in the bus with her and we went off four hours into the rural areas. We arrived at this community where indigenous Zulu healers were having a very special day. She wanted me to just be there to witness and participate. There were probably 300 villagers, and they were having a collective grief ritual as part of their regular community gatherings.

Once a month when they would gather, one of the elder healers would lead the ceremonies. They would begin with a song, the sounds of which still give me goosebumps. Soulful, deep, bluesy singing. Next the elder would instruct the people to go and collect a rock for every person they have ever lost. People came back with rocks. Some would have one. Some would have fifty. They placed them in a circle, or a community altar. Then people were invited to share.

I had never been to anything like this. Some people wailed for an hour and everyone joined them in their wailing. Some people told a story of their loss and everybody participated in the story. Kids were part of it. Elders were part of it. This lasted the whole day. Then afterward, they held a party with music and dance and food.

Here I witnessed Black, indigenous African peoples owning all the cultural rituals for moving through grief: remembering, memorializing, releasing.

It was one of the most profound teachings of my life. It shook me to realize how much we've lost in our colonization, and part of what we've lost is access to serious, important ways of grieving together in community.

Prudence was a profound teacher for me. For that time, for an HIV/AIDS leader on the African continent, writing into her grant proposals was considered completely scandalous.

I also remember something Prudence said in one of my first meetings with her: "Forty-nine of us started this organization. Forty-eight are dead. Every mess I create in my organization as an HIV-positive person living with AIDS is because I have not done enough of my grieving. It shows up in me being a messy leader."

There is so much pain to work out in our movements and in our own leadership. Prudence taught me that we have to remember and reinstitute those collective ways of bereavement.

Reflection

- What would new collective grief rituals that are free from colonized ideas of life and death look like?

- How can leaders take responsibility for holding and expressing the grief that so many hold, so that we can all continue our work?

Judging

Over the past six months or so I've noticed that I've become increasingly judgmental—always looking to establish who or what is right/wrong, good/bad, better/worse. Perhaps it is partly my human nature, but I'm sure it has been exacerbated by the schisms created by our collective discourse based on the false and toxic notion that we are inherently isolated from one another.

I was recently at the market, and in line ahead of me was a lovely woman. She chatted with the cashier, said hello to me when I got in line, and was sunny and very pleasant to be around. I thought "What a nice person! That's how we Oaklanders are." I felt good in her presence and judged her to be a fine person.

When I returned to my car I noticed that the van next to me had vitriolic anti-vax statements written on all the windows—complete with websites and condemnation. I was stunned by the quantity of it and thought "Wow! This person is really hateful—I hope they don't live in the neighborhood." I certainly wouldn't want them living next door to me.

I glanced over to see who the driver was, and sure enough, it was the woman who'd been in line in front of me. In my judgmental universe, this woman moved from neighbor to enemy in five short minutes. I went from delighted to outraged, while she was totally unaffected, simply going about the business of her day.

What a powerful lesson on how my judgments say everything about me and nothing about the person I'm judging. The only thing I can say for certain is that she was a very pleasant woman who drove a van covered with anti-vax language. She went home oblivious, and I went home angry and baffled, my adrenaline up and running.

I'm beginning to see how my judgments are taking a toll on me: it's exhausting to constantly monitor who the good people are, who have the wrong ideas, and so on. There is also a cost to those around me—I can become a bit cranky and short-tempered, and I'm sure my beloveds have noticed. This is not how I want to be in the world.

What if I simply let all that go, remembering that no one—not a single human in my lifetime—ever asked me to be the arbiter of human behavior. I've never been appointed to watch people from on high, and I can see that it is my mind and ego that are doing the judging. My heart and spirit really have no interest in taking on that onerous task.

When I consider letting go of being judge and jury, I can feel how big a burden I've been carrying. The energy I use to constantly monitor the thoughts and behaviors of others can be used for other things—like loving the people around me, delighting in a walk in the hills, or making dinner for a treasured friend. These things are so much more satisfying and remind me that I am inextricably connected to this earth and all life.

So I'm going to set down the burden of monitoring and judging others. I'm going to take up my particular work with a good and steady heart. This will be good for me, good for us, and good for our beautiful planet. I invite you to join me.

Reflection

- What burden may it be time to lay down?
- How does judging others take up your energy?
- What connects you to, rather than separates you from, others?

Taking out the trash

I was hosting a live webinar for more than 500 leaders. I was dressed up, hair done, and lipstick on. I was looking cute and everyone was tuning in. Great questions were being asked, and in the middle of dropping my wisdom, the door to my office opens and my mom walks in wearing pink flannel pajamas.

"It's trash day, and you forgot to take the trash out," she scolds.

"And also you haven't had any breakfast. Here's some food." She walks over to my desk, sets down a bowl of fruit, and closes the door.

This is the number one reason I have stayed intact as a leader. When I have told this story, people react immediately with, "How mortifying! Weren't you so embarrassed?" But in fact, no, I was not embarrassed because my mom's interruption that day was illustrative of a point I was trying to make to the group of leaders listening to the webinar that day: You have to find a way to remain completely humble to your own self. Maybe we can't be humble in the world, because we do have to play our positional power effectively to make change happen.

But we must know, in our heart of hearts, it doesn't matter who we think we are. I have a mom right there who's going to ask, "Why didn't you take the trash out?"

As leaders, we cannot mind taking out the trash if we are building a world where everybody's labor and dignity is valued. We can't build a beautiful vision if we don't have a clean house/office/workspace, right?

Often people new to movement leadership, who come from more formal corporate or institutional backgrounds, will say, "You're blowing my mind! You're willing to roll up your sleeves and do everything!" Most professionals can't even get access to executives without going through their assistants or scheduling systems. A lot of our traditional organizational leadership trains us to orient to, "Now you've 'made it.' Now your job is to give orders."

The most effective way that we have seen leaders lead is to do what needs to be done—whatever it is. This is even more important when there's fear among a team about doing something new. Taking people forward means modeling how to do it, step by step, ourselves first.

Reflection

- In what ways do you remain completely humble to yourself?

- How do you shy away from "taking out the trash," or doing what needs to be done?

Spinach on your teeth

We have learned the importance of building authentic relationships with other leaders who are willing to say, "I don't know what's going on and I don't know what to do."

We often refer to the circles of trust we build as "the kitchen table" because of the intimacy of "home" that is necessary. To tell the truth about our lives, to be witnessed within a web of care and accountability and generosity and mutuality is how we face another day. The kitchen table is a web of love and a circle of protection that allows you to explore ideas that may be uncomfortable or to take risks in an island of safety.

The kitchen table holds your innate trustworthiness and invests in the development of your innate wisdom. We offer feedback to each other that is not assaultive, even if it's not what we may want to hear. And as a result, the kitchen table is where we can derive strength, anytime.

Every single one of us needs trusted, beloved people who will not hesitate to say, "Girl, you got spinach on your teeth."

As we do the work of building a world where more people belong, we have to make sure that we too have a cherished place to belong.

Reflection

- Who is at your kitchen table?
- Who can you count on to name the spinach on your teeth?
- With whom do you belong?

Without reservation

After a period of fasting, Jains say *Michhami Dukadam* to each other. This is how it translates:

> *I forgive without any reservation all living beings who may have caused me any pain and suffering either in this life or previous lives, and I ask, without reservation, for forgiveness from all living beings, no matter how small or big, to whom I may have caused pain and suffering in this life or previous lives, knowingly or unknowingly, mentally, verbally, or physically. I begin the year with a clean slate, extending friendship to all living beings and animosity toward none.*

To practice this is harder than to read and be moved by these touching words. To forgive, without any reservation, to choose a clean slate when holding on to pain, anger, rage is so much more satisfying takes regular practice.

I am an amateur in this practice, but I take great solace in the fact that each year I will have a chance in this period to reflect on how I may make amends. This annual practice lightens the load and helps me show up more joyfully, more present, more loving toward my family, colleagues, and anyone else I encounter.

All scriptures have reminded us that ultimately, forgiveness frees us. It is not an act of benevolence toward others but an ultimate invitation toward our own freedom inside of our human interdependence.

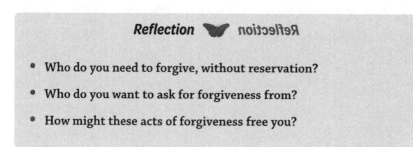

Reflection

- Who do you need to forgive, without reservation?
- Who do you want to ask for forgiveness from?
- How might these acts of forgiveness free you?

PRACTICE

Every leader makes mistakes—it's impossible not to. Sometimes we hurt those around us. We don't know a single human who is unscathed by some trauma.

When we refuse to forgive those who have "wronged" us we remain tethered to that person energetically, and that can drain our resources and tap our power. To forgive is liberating: it literally frees us and allows us to use our precious vital force and energy for the things and people who matter most to us.

Take a moment to consider if there is someone (or more than one) it might be time to forgive. What small step can you take in the direction of forgiveness? What might this free you up to do?

Take a moment to consider if there is someone from whom you need to ask forgiveness. What small step can you take?

When you are ready (and only then) we invite you to take those steps.

CHAPTER 5

Kindness, Trust, and Compassion

Choosing to be kind, to trust, and to exercise compassion is difficult especially when faced with the tensions in today's workplaces. And yet, without these essential ingredients, our leadership can fall prey to old notions of power and control. It takes courage indeed to operate from a place of kindness, trust, and compassion, especially when we may hear that for the sake of efficiency, it's best simply to exert suspicion, anger, and control. If our job as leaders is to bring everyone along and to remember that no one is easily dispensable, then we should practice exercising the discipline of kindness, compassion, and trust. This practice brings joy, for it expands our capacity to be fully human and creates safety for those who depend on our leadership. When people feel emotionally safe with one another, they have greater possibility for connection and joy.

The trivet

I was a hospice volunteer for several years, many years ago.

When my mother was dying, the hospital staff were astonishingly kind and compassionate. She and my whole family were so well cared for. I wanted to thank them in some tangible way, and in the 1990s, a hospice program opened here in Oakland. I'd heard that they were looking for volunteers, so I signed up.

Imagine me, a trained up and newly minted hospice volunteer with my shiny badge. I was ready.

I was sent to visit a dying woman who lived in Alameda, a place I'd never driven to before, but I could see on my way there that I had left the diverse town of Oakland. In any case, I arrived at a little six-unit apartment and rang the doorbell.

The woman who I later learned was the woman's daughter answered the door.

"I'm here, your hospice volunteer."

The daughter looked at me and said, "Oh . . . well, come in."

It was kind of a strange moment. She was warm, but her face clearly showed surprise.

I walked in and found an old woman, probably in her eighties, dying of cancer. I simply said, "Hello, I'm Akaya."

"I'm Vertha," she replied, but she stared at me with a look that said, "I don't know you. And you're in my house."

I looked back thinking, "Why are you giving me that attitude? I'm here to be helpful," while both of us sized up whether this would work.

My job as a volunteer was to offer family caregivers respite to enable them to run errands, do the laundry, or just have some time to themselves. The daughter, who was caring for her mother, said, "I'll be back in four hours."

So Vertha and I started to chat, uneasily at first, and then she said, "You know, I come from Norfolk, West Virginia. Do you know, Norfolk?"

"No, I've never been to West Virginia," I replied.

"Well, we used to have a saying when I was young," she said. "We are the girls from Norfolk, Norfolk. We don't dance. We don't drink. Nor folk. Nor folk."

I was taken aback for a moment, and then I fell in love with her. Who was this woman? She was hilarious! I just burst out laughing. And when I did, she burst out laughing too. At that moment, I thought, "Okay, this may work."

Over the course of about three months until her death, I spent four hours a week with Vertha. We established a friendship that crossed generations, races, classes—all of it. And at one point, she said to me, "You know, I was taught that Black people and white people shouldn't be friends."

"Yeah, I get that," I replied.

"But I can tell that maybe that is wrong."

"Well, clearly," I said.

"So now I know we can be friends. But I don't think that God intended that Black people and white people should marry and have children."

"Well, Vertha, my sister is married to a white man, and they have children, so clearly God intended that that could be rightful."

"Well, I just can't believe that God would want that."

"I'm sure that God wants my niece and my nephew."

She paused and said, "Well, you may be right. And maybe it's time for people who think like me to die."

What I didn't say was, "Yeah, damn skippy!"

What I said instead was, "May be . . . may be."

I went to see Vertha the week before she died. It was the last time I was to see her. When I arrived, she said, "Akaya, I've been going through my things, and I put something for you in the kitchen."

"You did?"

"You go on in there. It's on the counter."

Vertha collected clowns, figurines, all kinds of items. She loved clowns, and they were all over her house. I walked into the kitchen, and on the counter was a ceramic trivet. On it was a clown in blackface, on his knee, in the mammy stance.

I thought to myself, "I have a choice to make. I can receive this from my political side, which sees this as hateful, racist propaganda. Or I can receive this from my 'This is from Vertha, who is doing her best' side."

I chose the latter. This gift was from her heart, so I chose to receive it in my heart.

I was very glad that the trivet was in the kitchen and not at her side, so that I had a moment to collect myself. I took a deep breath and thought, "Okay, I need to give her a real response."

I walked back in the room with her and said, "Vertha, I'm touched. I'm really touched by this."

To which she said, "Do you like it?"

"I will always treasure this," I replied.

"Oh, I'm so glad because my daughter said she wasn't sure. She said you might not like it."

"You tell her it's just fine. Thank you."

"I'm so glad. I'm *so* glad—I saved it just for you."

I still have that trivet. It is in my basement, in a box that nobody sees. But I know exactly where it is, and I will have that trivet for the rest of my days. That trivet is a reminder that even in the last moments of our lives, we can change.

I'm so grateful to have witnessed Vertha taking the journey from "I don't believe that Black people and white people could be friends" to questioning what God intended, and then understanding that it was time for people like her to go. In three months, that's a lot of movement.

I'm also grateful that Spirit brought us together because I, too, needed to change. It was an important lesson to see myself at a crossroads between my political stance and my spiritual side, which are both useful and necessary, but which sometimes come into conflict.

Vertha invited me to choose our shared humanity over my politics. I'm very glad I did.

Reflection

- Leaders often must make choices based on political purity, or humanity and relatedness. How do you do so when they don't fit nicely into the same circle?

- What makes you choose to keep your heart open? How do you create flexibility for nuance?

- Who can support you through the most intimate and intense of losses? Who is willing to be present in the muck of grief with you?

Kinship

Flying home from a conference I had the good luck of sitting in the exit row with an empty seat beside me. I was tired from all the talking and engagement and was very much looking forward to a few hours of silence and down time.

At the last possible moment, the flight attendants seated a weepy, sniffling, and obviously miserable woman next to me. My heart sank as my irritation rose. Was I going to have to sit beside a whimpering person all the way home? I turned to my magazine and pretended that I didn't notice her suffering.

After about five minutes, the better part of me won out over the less evolved part of me, and I somewhat grumpily turned to her and asked if she needed anything. She told me that her twenty-year-old grandson had just been accidentally shot in the head. He was in the hospital, barely clinging to life. Her name was Doris, and she was all alone as she desperately tried to get to him. My heart softened, I put away my magazine, and I offered her my hand. The passenger on the other side of her is a friend and colleague of mine who, having overheard Doris's story, took her other hand as well.

The three of us sat, for three and a half hours, praying and holding and talking about life. We kept company, as all kindred should in these kinds of situations.

At one point, Doris talked about the shooting, and I said, "I hate guns—I want every gun to disappear from the planet."

She looked at me blankly and said, "Guns don't kill people! That's like saying that pencils are responsible for education."

I thought, "What the heck?! How can it be that she is desperately trying to get to her obviously beloved grandson who is possibly dying from a gunshot and defend the use of guns?" I knew this was not the moment to get into that discussion, but I was flummoxed by the seeming disconnect between her values and her personal experience.

Doris also mentioned that she lives in Mitch McConnell's district, and I noticed that I began to construct a story about who she might be. This story put us on distinctly disparate parts of the political spectrum, and it occurred to me that under any other circumstance, we might have little in common, and even less to talk about.

In this moment, however, the wisdom of the heart eclipsed the politics of the mind. Differences in agenda, point of view, strategy, and geography ceased to matter. Here was a woman named Doris, a person whose grief I shared, who needed a hand in a difficult time.

While we in the social change world often come together and unite in like-minded causes for social, racial, and economic justice, we rarely commune or share with those "on the other side." This experience moved me to ask myself: What would happen if we stretched across boundaries and differences to acknowledge our collective humanity truly and deeply—even if we are on opposite sides of a divided issue?

Mary McLeod Bethune once wrote, "Leadership is the capacity to respond to what's needed in the moment." Doris, who is now among my kin, needed my tenderness, not my judgment. Leadership often asks us to set aside our assumptions and our biases in order to do what's needed. I learned this once again on a plane traveling west, heading home.

Reflection

- When have your politics and compassion been at odds?
- When, as a leader, might you need to choose politics over compassion?
- When, as a leader, might you need to choose compassion over politics?

When we listen to the grandmothers

I took my first toxic tour of South Durban, South Africa, in 2012. Hosted by the South Durban Community Environmental Alliance (SDCEA), an organization led by Goldman Prize winner Desmond D'Sa, the purpose of the tour was to learn from community members how they were holding the most egregious corporate polluters accountable in their neighborhoods, in South Africa, and beyond.

I sat in a room with a grandmother who had learned the bucket method to test and monitor air quality. She was part of the "bucket brigade," or SDCEA's signature low-tech, high-impact way for community members to collect air samples for identifying pollutants.

For her, having grandchildren drop out of school due to asthma was no longer acceptable. She knew that Black and Brown children who did not complete school would soon join a permanent underclass of oppressed service sector workers. For her own grandchildren and for the dream of liberation of all people, she took it upon herself to show up at every chemical leak or flare in her community. She would be there to do the research and to educate, inform, and organize more people.

As a student of movement building, that day I learned about the power of responsiveness. When your community is struggling every single day to breathe, your organization does not have the luxury to plan a meeting two months down the road.

I learned that you always begin from where you are. You make information available and accessible so that every grandmother can imbibe it with ease and use it to transform herself into a changemaker.

SDCEA also helped me see that you do not let the size of your budget determine the magnitude of your impact. With complete commitment, D'Sa and colleagues on the toxic tour talked about how together we would stop port expansion in South Durban, which would displace people and cause even more toxic pollution in South Africa's "Cancer Alley." Together we would get our message to the

South African government and their international financiers. We would name and shame all those implicated in displacing thousands of our people in this neo-apartheid time.

A few years later, I got to watch as SDCEA and its partners did, in fact, stop the Durban port expansion dead in its tracks. SDCEA and local communities managed to deploy a strategic mix of advocacy and organizing to ensure that there was a groundswell of resistance combined with de-legitimization of the expansion project.

If SDCEA, with its grassroots base and small budget (proportionate to big philanthropy), can do all this to achieve climate justice, then why not us?

Imagine a future where we could be as responsive, community aligned, feisty, and prepared as SDCEA. We do not build progressive dreams on merely an idealistic, aspirational perspective, but on conviction grounded in many decades of walking alongside "bucket brigade" grandmothers and supporting many more of the fiercest community-led actions in the world.

When grandmothers become community scientists, when neighborhoods unite across race and class differences, when grassroots groups create movement infrastructure, and when funders collaborate with each other and with movements in solidarity, we—all of us—make climate justice possible.

Reflection

- How do you prioritize responsiveness to people on the front lines of their community?

- Who are the effective leaders in your community you can develop or support?

- How are you contributing to an interconnected global climate justice movement at this time?

None of us are islands

As beings, none of us are islands.

Natural ecological systems or ecosystems demonstrate to us that we survive and thrive because of the interactions between species and elements. This is such an important lesson for all of us working to advance social justice.

Around the world the social movements and organizations we support on the front lines of change in their communities are increasingly taking lessons from ecosystems as well. They work in powerfully decentralized ways. For example, La Via Campesina is an international movement working at scale with more than 200 million smallholder farmers and peasants globally. The movement is not focused on elevating a singular charismatic leader but rather works as a coalition of more than 150 organizations.

Let us never forget that local systems and organized grassroots groups exist in *all* parts of the world. They are already addressing the most intractable challenges of climate change, rising inequality, and failing food systems. We need not parachute in to solve people's problems but ask: What is underfunded? How can we be of greatest use?

Around the world, grassroots solutions tend to emerge when leaders on the ground draw from and share indigenous, contextual, and collective expertise. They come from making deeper connections to the natural world and from working directly with families as they cope with the unequal burdens and chaos created by the climate crisis and other systemic injustices.

For grassroots activists in the Global South who bravely stand up to challenge climate destruction or call for climate-wise alternatives, their activism is being met with increasing repression and violence. As movement leaders in the United States have faced heightened risks, threats of violence, and increased dangers from state repression, vigilante violence, and cyberattacks, killings of people protecting environmental and land rights across the Global South are also increasing. Quite literally, many of our planet's most luminous climate heroines and heroes are being violently taken from their work and beloved communities, often with impunity and with woefully inadequate action by the international community.

Standing with and investing resources in local initiatives ensures a readiness for change, as well as ownership of the change process itself. It reflects cultural, social, political, geographic, and economic realities—a nuance of understanding that outsiders cannot possess. At the same time, we all need the diversity and strength of leadership and solutions offered by grassroots actors around the world.

To embody an ecosystem approach in our work means focusing on building power in communities, creating fierce strategies to change systems, and activating the power of advocacy and grassroots organizing for lasting social change. Grassroots organizing not only wins change at the local level but, in case after case, builds the political pressure and context for national, regional, and international change as well.

Because none of us are islands.

Reflection

- Who/what is your ecosystem?
- How might you lead to benefit the whole ecosystem?

PRACTICE

There is a distinct difference between niceness and kindness—what is it?

Many of us were taught as children to be nice: to make others comfortable, to go along even when we know something is off. Niceness teaches us to ignore a problem, to not speak when what we say may cause friction or discord. Niceness teaches us to lie.

Kindness, on the other hand, allows us to recognize that even when we disagree, we are all kin. If we go back far enough, every single one of us is related to everyone else. If we acknowledge and remember this link of kinship, we can say the hardest of things while keeping everyone's humanity in the center of our hearts and minds. Kindness also builds trust among and between people—niceness can divide us.

Take a moment and notice what might be possible if you refused to be nice and always reached for kindness and compassion. What might you risk? What might you gain?

We invite you to spend the next two weeks being kind (perhaps not an easy thing to do in these troubled times). When you feel yourself slipping into niceness, pause. Take a breath, reset, and ground yourself in your heart of kindness, remembering that you're talking with a relative.

Two weeks of leading from a place of kindness—we'd be interested in hearing what you learn.

CHAPTER 6

Grief, Challenge, and Disappointment

The good news is that we are all learning and growing. The challenging news is that we are all learning and growing, and that means we will make mistakes, fall down, and occasionally mess things up completely. People leave, organizations fail, and opportunities are lost. It is important that we as leaders acknowledge our mistakes and allow for grief and disappointment. If we do this, we learn, subsequently grow, and become wiser. This is a marvelous thing indeed. When we eventually pick ourselves up and continue to practice, each "mistake" becomes a learning/growing step, which is essential on a joyful path.

Rose-colored glasses

Years back, there was a young woman on my staff. I saw so much potential for her leadership and I steadily mentored her, encouraged her, gave her new opportunities to grow, opened doors for her, and gently pushed her along her path to become the stellar leader I thought she could be.

After several years, it became apparent to me that she just

couldn't or wouldn't walk through those doors. Either she wasn't ready or perhaps she simply didn't want to be what I had assumed she should be.

This disappointed me greatly, and we had to have an honest conversation that perhaps she might find a better fit in a new leadership role in another organization. This was the last thing either of us wanted. We ended up going our separate ways, and it's a wound that has never fully been healed—though I'm happy to report she is thriving in her new position, and I'm sure our time together helped contribute to her role as a leader today.

In reflecting on my own role as a leader/mentor in this relationship, I realized that I needed to acknowledge my part of it. Had I seen her for her own realistic potential? Was I building a role for something she was actually capable of? Or even wanted? Why was I pushing her to be who she wasn't?

I am an optimist and I often see life through rose-colored glasses. That said, I've also come to understand that I can miss the real capacities and desires of those around me if I only see them through my lens. This isn't fair.

Here's a conundrum—we may be able to see a spark in someone that they cannot yet see. We wouldn't be who we are as leaders if we didn't have high hopes and aspirations for the people that we lead.

I'm still an optimist and will always continue to provide leadership opportunities to those who want them. But I now know that when I take the time and space to truly see a person in their wholeness, this also means I may have to sit with my own disappointment when someone doesn't meet my expectations.

When I own those feelings, I'm less likely to superimpose them on others. I do not have the right to make someone "wrong" for being who they are and where they are on their journey.

Reflection

- How do we recognize both the potential *and* the reality of a person's capacity for leadership?

- When has a person not met your expectations for them? How did you handle being let down?

Good grief

For many years I was a volunteer at one of our local hospice organizations. I visited with folks on their last journey, giving their caregivers a bit of a break. During that time I learned a lot about death, dying, and the process of grieving.

Recently, a colleague told me that for the past year she's been feeling like there has been a death in the family. She gave words to what I've been feeling as well. I realize that I've been going through the steps of grief: anger, disbelief, denial, depression, and the rest. There is still a part of me that thinks I'll wake up tomorrow and life will return to "normal." It won't, and that's both good news and bad.

The vast majority of the people in the United States have never been served by systems that degrade, isolate, and dehumanize us. The good news could be that seeing this truth writ large and loud allows us to approach social transformation with fresh eyes, hearts, and ideas. The hard news is that the comfortable little bubble of my former "normal life" is no longer available to me, which in the long run, is good news.

A lot of folks have been grieving—a reasonable response to the specter of hate-filled racialized and gendered violence and massive COVID deaths. It is wise that we allow ourselves the time and space to notice and respond to this historical moment. It is equally wise that we understand that others are also grieving and that we offer them tenderness, compassion, and empathy. This is not a time to turn on each other, it is a time to turn toward each other.

I've been watching as leaders making change lash out at each other, and I think we can do better than that. People are hurting, but rather than lashing out at each other because of differences in strategy, political approach, or analysis, what if we let each other be for a while? It is so easy to turn our dismay on one another, but that's not the way of transformation. If someone wants to march in the streets, or write a song or a manifesto, get a massage or binge-watch TV, let them! There is no "right" way to face this moment. The path of grief is neither linear nor rational and judging others for the way they are responding is not going to get us where we want to go. Let's decide as family to hold off our debating and continue to try and stay connected.

Poco a poco, we'll be coming to terms with a changed socio-political context. In some ways I could argue that this moment is what so many of us (and those who have come before us) have been working toward: the breakdown of oppressive empire and the concomitant opportunity of new possibilities. One of my biggest points of grief was realizing that this process of transformation will undoubtedly be chaotic and dangerous. Naïve on my part, perhaps, but dismaying nonetheless.

In the coming months we will collectively decide how to respond (and not solely react). Some of us will choose to oppose, resist, agitate, and interrupt; others will dream up new ideas and create new life-centered ideologies. Some will sing, make art, or dance in the streets, while others will pray and guide and tend the gardens. Doesn't matter what it is, we need it all. We need every heart, mind, hand, and soul willing to do the hard work of ushering in the new era.

From where I sit, I can see that despite what might unravel in the coming several years, we are in excellent hands in the long run. We will get through this moment and figure out our next big collective steps toward evolution. My conversations with leaders among Generation X and Millennials assure me of this.

Let's take the time we need to grieve—and this will be different for each of us. Allowing ourselves to grieve is crucial in the work of transformation. This is not the best of times nor is it the worst. We'll get through this—our ancestors have proven this time and again, and the generations coming along will surely lead the way.

Reflection 🦋 noitɔɘlʇɘЯ

- What are you grieving these days?

- Are you giving yourself the time to sit with your feelings?

- How are you responding to this particular moment?

Undone

Young women will often ask me, "What's the path to get to be you? What did you do to have your life?"

I respond by starting at the place I was years and years ago: I was a hot mess. I was in a difficult intimate relationship. I had chronic back pain. I was barely able to function.

I knew that part of it was that I was in a really toxic work environment. I had an awful boss and a fancy high-rise office that overlooked a beautiful vista that I knew made my parents proud when they came to visit from India. I was making the most money I've ever made.

Yet literally every morning when I got out of bed, a feeling of dread would wash over me. I would tell myself, "You 'made it,' and little girls from Rajasthan don't often make it, so you better suck it up and go to work!"

In all of my confusion and despair, when I was trying to decide whether to quit my high-paying social enterprise job for a grassroots nonprofit job, I went to see an old and dear friend. She probed about the real decision I was trying to make.

"Walk me through your ideal day," she said.

That was her only prompt to me. She didn't offer advice. She simply wanted to know what the picture of my ideal day looked like, hour by hour, from waking to sleeping.

I remember telling her, "I wake up. I make love with my partner. Then we drink coffee in bed. Then I do an hour of yoga. And then I work from my garden. Then I make beautiful food and eat it while breathing. I do creative and strategic work then go to bed knowing that I was part of something so much bigger than myself."

At the time she asked me this question, despite my fabulous salary and office, I was living in a tiny studio apartment where there was no garden. My partner and I woke up every morning and we'd fight for hours. I would go to work hungover or over-caffeinated.

Nothing of what I was describing to my friend that day was in any way close to the life I was leading.

By the time I got to describing the end of my ideal day, I realized that everything in my life needed to change, not just the job. I knew what I was saying would necessitate deep changes in my orientation to work, home, love, health. It was hard to admit this because I didn't know where to start. So much needed attention.

I started with the job piece as one way to start. I let myself say yes to a job that filled my heart, even if it cut my pay in half. From there, I took the next step, then the next step, and then the next, all of which took me out of my comfort zone.

My life now is pretty much aligned to that picture I painted for my friend that day. But to get here, there were many colonial and capitalist patterns I had to break about what I had been taught a "successful life" looks like.

I also learned that sometimes you just have to accept that you're going to be undone before you can come together again.

And it's worth it.

Reflection  noitɔɘʅʅɘЯ

- **What must you undo to truly thrive?**
- **What is your ideal day?**
- **What's one step today toward that day?**

…and sometimes it's just freaking hard

Recently, four friends of mine lost parents and siblings, and even though all were expected, it's still hard. COVID, isolation, and economic insecurity are rampant, and many organizations are having a challenging time. The instability of our national government in recent years has made it really hard for many folks.

I come from a family that lived by the adage "God bless the child who's got his own." I learned early and thoroughly not to complain, to toughen up and deal, and to do what's in front of me right now and with excellence. There was kindness in my family, but we were expected to do our part without much help and to get it done well. It was the way my parents learned to survive, and I honor that they passed those lessons on to me. In many ways, those lessons have allowed me to be successful in my work, but they also taught me that I must be totally self-reliant and not depend on anyone else—that fundamentally I can only count on myself to do things right.

And that's what makes things hard. Unnecessarily so.

A while ago, I was having one of "those" days, so I called Rajasvini and asked her to remind me why I said yes to this work.

Without missing a beat, she said, "Because you are born for it. You have a gift for it. You love it and no one is better suited for it."

My jaw dropped. I was expecting her to join me in a bit of "woe is me" and instead she showered me with a deep and affirmative truth I needed to hear. A truth I wasn't capable of telling myself at that moment.

She lovingly yanked me out of my isolation and put me right smack back into the circle of relatedness.

I could not have done that alone. It was a reminder of how much I need others if I am to be effective and work over a lifetime. It was a reminder of how much each of us needs each of us—we cannot do the work of transforming the world unless we are in an interdependent relationship, the work is too vast and complex for any one of us.

I had to defy my early training even to reach out to my friend, and I am grateful to her for not colluding with my "woe is me." Since that day, I've looked for other ways to practice reaching out and asking for help, and I've been astonished by the many folks who are delighted to lend a hand, a shoulder, or some much-needed wisdom. Wow!

Leadership can be downright daunting at times. The next time life feels hard, I invite you to reach out and see who responds. I'll bet there is more support for each of us than we can imagine. I'm beginning to wonder how much of the isolation many leaders feel is based in a false belief that we are alone.

Let's reach toward each other. Let's ask for assistance when we need it and lend a hand when we can. I promise you that the work of transforming the world will be much more satisfying, effective, and less hard if we do it together.

Reflection

- What were some of your early lessons about asking for help?
- Who around you is struggling and could use some help?

The encounter

They had persevered against threats of assassination, constant harassment, grave personal losses, and surveillance. From Nigeria and Brazil, they have peacefully organized their communities against the collusion of corporate and governmental powers that seek to cause harm to Mother Earth. They were people who have fought for decades to preserve the land, water, forests, territories, and cultural knowledge of Indigenous and rural peoples.

I was honored to have the chance to moderate a public conversation with these brilliant environmental defenders and warriors for justice at a major social impact conference, in a session attended by more than 100 people.

After the event ended, an older white gentleman, who has many decades of board membership of several human rights organizations and past political wins under his belt, approached me. Let's call him Mike. Mike proceeded to berate me for not giving him sixty precious seconds to launch his "new" idea for a philanthropic fund at the event.

"How could you ignore me? Clearly, you are not serious about moving resources to defenders. I was here to help, but you made it impossible," said Mike.

I explained that with so many questions and only twenty minutes for our Q & A session, it simply was not possible to entertain all the raised hands, and in his case, he never raised his hand to speak. It felt more important to be equitable across the room and get as many questions directed to the panelists as possible. In an attempt to de-escalate the vitriol aimed at me, which was shocking after a rather successful event and discussion, I asked Mike if he would like to share his ideas in a follow-up email with those gathered.

Upon hearing this, Mike became enraged. He raised his voice and told me that he was a very important man. He simply did not have time to engage in emails.

"The ball is in your court. If you want my attention, you will write to me. I cannot promise I have time to respond to all the emails I get from people like you," said Mike.

I explained to him that funds like the ones he proposes already exist. In fact, one of the members of the CLIMA (Climate Leaders in Movement Action) Fund collaborative—the Urgent Action Fund for Women's Human Rights—is particularly skilled at getting rapid-response funds into the hands of environmental defenders within twenty-four hours.

Mike was so carried away by his righteous rage that he did not listen to a word I was saying. Instead he continued to make the case for his importance, my mistake in not honoring his singular idea, and the serious implications this could have for me. I explained I was not interested in seeking his funds—that I was doing my job as a moderator on this panel.

"And I lead a foundation, a grantmaking organization, that already does what you want to start to do," said I.

Mike continued his diatribe. I felt my blood pressure rising. And my heart sinking.

I excused myself to attend to the many people who were moved by our event and wanted to share their thanks and reflections with me. I took three breaths. I attended to the task at hand—to connect and build with the many people in the room who came with minds and hearts ready to learn and to honor environmental defenders.

The audience had just finished pairing up in an engaging dialogue about how we are complicit in the threats that face defenders. With communities facing such loss of land and lives, many people in attendance were grappling with questions of how best to exercise solidarity. People wanted to talk more about how we may act in our own backyards to stop the financing of extractive industries and to block policies that perpetuate killings of environmental defenders.

I walked away from Mike, this caricature of a failing empire asserting itself in its own importance. I walked away from Mike, who needed to place himself at the top of a crumbling hierarchy when encountering the brilliant collective power of people of color and people from the Global South.

I believe Mike's frustration represents a social-good industry trying to find its relevance as more women, especially from formerly colonized countries, are rising to leadership. Global development and international philanthropy used to be a sector that ensured that we knew our place only as junior staff—middle management the most for which we could hope.

I wish I could say this was a surprise. I wish I could say I have never had to ignore racist, misogynistic, offensive bullies before. But sadly, it was not. I walked away with clarity as well as sadness.

Clarity that when I said I represented the CLIMA Fund—a collaboration of four fierce organizations all led by women who are seeking to solve the climate crisis not singularly but collectively—that it is still hard to believe that such a thing can exist. It must intimidate Mike that we do not ride on celebrity charisma or patriarchal displays of importance, but instead work thoughtfully with each other through complementary strengths and with accountability to environmental defenders, climate justice activists, grassroots organizations, social movements, and aligned advocates.

Sadness that in our search for meager resources to fund our partners' under-resourced work, we are willing to make accommodations for Mikes and the possibility of their support in the form of money, media, and connections. Sad that the implicit bias inside Mike made him assume that I am yet another woman of color without power. Sad that that bias led him to treat me with disrespect and paternalism. Sad that it took Mike realizing that I am a funder to soften his stance.

Later as I was talking with a climate scientist, Mike interrupted my conversation to assert himself once again. He handed me his business card and said, "I might have come across as being cross. Here's my card. If you write to me and I'm not too busy, I may respond."

I wrote to Mike. I wrote to him to invite him to talk more with me about how his misdirected frustration impacted me; if his espoused values are congruent with his actions; how he would train his own daughter to respond if a man came at her the way he did at me; to examine what insecurity or fear was at play for him that prevented him from deeply listening to the solutions offered by people of color and women on the stage; and why he must invent something anew when so much already exists that he could support and help grow.

I wrote to Mike because I believe in human transformation.

I did so because of the lessons I have been taught by grassroots leaders who put their lives on the line to fight for what they love: that we must invite all humans—with love—to become our comrades.

I did so because of what one of the panelists reminded our audience—including Mike and myself—that day. He, who has escaped many attempts on his life for his convictions in Nigeria, reminded us, "Once you are hooked to the struggle for justice, there's no going back!"

Reflection

- Who do you encounter that deflates you?
- How do you center yourself when encountering racism, ableism, ageism, sexism, classism?
- How do you choose to respond to encounters that hurt you?

The recovery

Before I could write to "Mike" following his belligerent and hostile public treatment of me, here is what I needed to recover:

I needed to share my story with my trusted beloveds and let them soothe my hurting heart over phone calls and several drinks.

I needed to feel my own rage, sadness, hurt, grief, and impatience.

I needed to know that I could look white supremacy and misogyny in its eyes and not let it destroy me.

I needed to talk to my trusted white friends and ask them for advice.

I needed to go on a walk with my older desi feminist sister leader and hear her guidance.

I needed to know that I am not alone.

Yes, over two decades of professional life as a leader of color, and I still have to pick myself up from the floor and piece myself together after every hurtful encounter with unchecked racism and sexism. I do so because I know power does not concede without confrontation, without organized demands, and without our capacity to engage with it.

I am determined to be unafraid of power.

I am determined to wield it with care and to change the conditions, as well as the narrative, about to whom power rightfully belongs.

I am determined to use my own influence, privilege, and networks to support Indigenous, Black, immigrant women, and gender queer people to lead with values and principles.

I am determined to remain accountable to the movements, leaders, and ancestors before us that made it possible for us to have this power.

I am hooked, I admit. I am hooked to not being another Brown woman who internalizes her own oppression, who exercises complicity through collegiality, who vents to her own community but remains compartmentalized at work. I refuse to be fragmented as a human and as a woman.

This is the work—the work of healing my heart; of asking for support; of speaking truth to power; and most of all, transforming conditions from abuse and extraction, toward greater harmony and interconnection.

If someone like me who can exercise relative privilege can be bruised and battered, what is the hope for the many young women of color who must still continue to work in organizations led by the self-important Mikes of the world?

This is why I always know I have to dust myself off and get to work.

Reflection

- What is your relationship to power?

- What do you do to "pick yourself up from the floor and piece yourself together" after painful encounters with people or harmful situations that lay bare the impacts of oppression?

When friends disappoint

After my dealings with "Mike" I experienced all of the somatic responses. I felt disassociated. I felt crazy. I felt a little bit of self-hate creeping in. I felt a deep fear of the repercussions for my organization.

As I was recovering, I went for a walk to clear my head and ran into a friend.

As I saw her, I thought, "It'd be so good to talk to my friend, the other person of color funder here."

We started walking together, and I recounted for her the whole gut-wrenching story. Her reaction was, "Sorry that happened to you. What's on the next panel tomorrow?"

I felt gutted again.

She wasn't being callous. Her reaction wasn't uncaring or competitive. What it communicated to me was that she didn't really want to pursue this line of thinking and analysis.

I realized later that she didn't want to engage with my story because in doing so she might have to confront the ways in which she makes compromises in her leadership. Was she thinking, "Oh, I would not have called this white man out the way Vini did"? Was she wondering what my story meant for her and how she stands up for herself, or not? Was she avoiding the pain she's also felt when she'd had similar experiences?

This encounter with Mike was so awful, so public, and so high-stakes. My heart broke again when I felt like my compañera bailed on me. To mend my heart, I had to remember, we all handle the pain of racism and its many forms in different ways.

Reflection 🦋 noitɔɘʃɘЯ

- **When did a friend or ally break your heart?**
- **How do you seek to mend your heart?**

Not just lunch

"Can you believe they passed me over?"

One of my Achilles' heels is that because of my cultural training, I have a lot of respect for elders. When somebody is twenty years my senior, my first impulse is to trust them.

When the leader of a larger foundation, an older white woman who traveled in the social justice spaces I did and was connected to a trusted friend, took an interest in taking me to lunch twice a year or so, I said yes.

It took me a while to understand why she was asking.

Our lunches were pleasant enough, but often our entire meetings would be about her lamenting the leadership jobs she applied for and did not get. In her way, she was soliciting my advice.

At first, I was understanding, "Yeah, that must be hard," because she had so much experience. I too wondered why she was not being seen, and felt that her experience must be really hurtful.

Then there was a moment when I saw these exchanges for what they were worth.

I had just accepted my new job, and she again invited me to a supposed congratulatory lunch, saying, "This is great news! I'm so proud of you."

Despite her declaration of support, at the restaurant she asked me, "Why you? When people like me exist with so much experience and a lifelong commitment to justice?"

Then in this congratulatory lunch, she began to tell me about how hard my new job was going to be because I didn't have enough years under my belt.

I finally realized that she was jealous. I saw right through her, and I let myself get angry. I remember thinking,

"You don't even *know* what I'm about to do. I don't need you. We are trying to build something entirely new that you could learn from!"

I asked myself: What's the lesson in this for my leadership? I realized that this story held the last vestiges of "I'm just a little girl from India who somehow 'found' herself in this position. And I just need my elders to support me."

I had to let go of the idea that every self-appointed mentor wants to see me thrive. That because we shared values nominally, that we would then share a commitment to embodying and living from that place. Only those who are fully resolved and intact in themselves can lift up other people. I had to get clearer about the people I turn to for guidance, advice, and mentorship.

Reflection  noitɔǝʅɟǝЯ

- When do you find yourself "convincing" yourself of someone's alignment with your interests, even when you have evidence to the contrary?
- What self-imposed inadequacy in yourself must you shed in order to lead powerfully?

PRACTICE

It can be very tempting to react swiftly when things go awry, to lash out, or jump to making a plan, or tell someone the "TRUTH!"

What if, when we find ourselves triggered by an event or person we stop. Literally stop, come to stillness, take a breath and center ourselves, and only after that ask, "What are my options here? What might be best for all concerned?" It might be easy to react swiftly, but that rarely gets us the results we want, and almost always creates more mess in the long run. Every leader we know, including ourselves, gets triggered now and again. It's part of human nature. While we can't control becoming triggered, we do have agency in what we do when triggered. If we come back to stillness and balance, we can respond rather than react, and our decisions will be more considered, considerate, and wise.

The next time you find yourself getting triggered (and that will inevitably happen) we invite you to notice that you're triggered, pause, breathe, come to stillness, and only after that ask, "How might I need/want to respond?"

Interrupting our knee-jerk patterns of reactivity is challenging work, but we believe it is essential if we want to be effective and trustworthy leaders.

CHAPTER 7

Keeping the Circle
Whole and Healthy

Making and building community is a matter of practice. Choosing to keep our circles of connection whole and healthy takes daily and mindful practice. If we are to create joyful internal cultures in our organizations, networks, alliances where every person is valued and nurtured, we will need to work *and* play! We can't create powerful and healthy ecosystems by simply muscling through tensions and stressors. Instead, a little lightness, a little joy, a little love, and a little mutual care go a long way in ensuring that our workplaces and our community groups become places where everyone can belong. We invite you to abandon any linear plans for development for just a moment, and wildly and playfully engage in the joyful practice of keeping the circle healthy and whole.

Small but essential

I have a strong commitment to living a life of gratitude for everything—even things I do not prefer or understand. My commitment to this overarching gratitude has been challenged by the presence of the coronavirus, and so I'm curious about the role of viruses in relationship to human life. I've been pondering their possible purpose in the large scheme of things.

Many of our cultural, economic, religious, and political institutions teach us to see ourselves as rulers over all dominion—that we have the right to shape the world in whatever way we choose. Our powers to make, influence, and destroy our ecosystem appears to have no limit. This is a toxic and very distorted way of thinking.

As I ponder the purpose of viruses, I wonder if they will be the force that puts borders on our capacity to rape and pillage this remarkable and singular earth. We clearly need constraints, and viruses seem uniquely suited to stay several steps ahead of us.

While I'm very attached to my particular life, at the same time I'm aware that I am only one among billions. Sometimes I sit and reflect on the fact that in a mere 125 years, every human extant will no longer exist. It's as if the human race has a chance to begin anew every century and a quarter or so. The anguishes and triumphs of this day will fade into the vast weave of human history, perhaps only to be remembered by the few who care to look back. This is a gift.

In the vastness of the universe, humans don't matter more than any other particular expression of life. What matters is our collective humanity—what we do as a species. What matters is how we understand and live as a collective among other collectives, how we fit into the interlocking circles of nematodes and oxen and flamingoes and pears.

I believe that as a species we are growing in our comprehension that we are only a small but essential part of the Whole. Some of our cultures have known this for millennia and others are slowly catching up. One of these days, and hopefully soon, our awareness of our place in the fabric of life will grow enough that we will interrupt our unhinged belief that we are special and therefore "above" the rest.

No one person matters more than any other one—every single one of us is worthy and precious. If we remember this, we can shift our thinking and behaviors. Even if we aren't sure what to do, we can begin learning and practicing now—let's call it global neighborliness. Reach out to a neighbor you may not know and ask what they might need. Donate to the food bank or animal shelter. Call your elders to see how they are. Even in a time of social spaciousness, refuse to separate emotionally, psychologically, or spiritually. Remember that we have no separate interests, that our individual well-being depends on the health of the forests and rivers, and that human life is inextricably connected to all life.

Let's breathe and practice and learn. Then breathe and practice and learn again, and then show the way for others. We can do this because it is one of our gifts as humans.

Hopefully the generations coming can and will lead us to an increasingly greater consciousness of interconnected life and will know how to live accordingly. If not, then I'm looking to our viral kindred to remind us that we are not kings, but a simple and necessary small piece of the whole living system.

What might be possible if we were to trust what's happening even if we don't understand it, and to look out for each other as we collectively travel through uncertain terrain? None of us can do this alone, but together we can create a future born of an ever-increasing awareness of our place in the family of things.

This will be good for us, good for our great-great-great-great-grands, and good for all life on our precious earth. For this I am grateful.

Reflection   🦋   noitɔelɟeᴿ

- Notice how you fit in the web of all life. What gift are you uniquely here to bring?

- What would change if you led with a steady awareness of interconnection?

- When did you first notice that you were worthy and precious?

Part of the whole

"How do I start a movement?"

This is a question I hear far too often.

You don't actually start a movement. No one does.

None of us wake up one day and say, "I'm gonna start a movement, and I'm gonna follow this prescription."

Movements, by their very definition, are about organized groups of people building power. There are various kinds of actors and actions within movements. Lots of pockets of organized groups of people, connected to each other, in a wider ecosystem, working for justice and building something together is truly a movement.

Movements are made by people coming around an idea and a vision to actually transform their very real material conditions. No one organization is a movement, and organizations don't start or build movements, people do. Organizations can provide a scaffold and accompany and support the people, but they can't *be* the movement. Without social movements, I don't believe you get social change.

People who want to be seen as movement leaders have to go out and build bases within their communities, build power at local and regional levels. They have to do what it takes to transform policy, to get people elected, to actually see systems change. Let the work guide you into how to grow it to a movement.

The greatest privilege of my job is that I'm trusted and that my organization has shown itself to be trustworthy. What this means is we get to have a peek into how people are working and organizing and strategizing. Then we get to bring our piece of the work—financial resources—and it actually is really beneficial. And . . . sometimes resources are not the most salient thing. It's about posing the fundamental question about what's most important right now.

Unfortunately, very few organizations are oriented that way, and many are not equipped to surface and navigate this tension.

An ecosystem approach to leadership, however, means weaving and connecting multiple external relationships. Essentially, you're getting people to work together, which is vastly different from leadership focused on competitive advantage or establishing exclusivity.

Honoring our place in the ecosystem is what being a leader within movements is. It's about finding where we are most helpful, because we have built relationships that show us what is most salient and needed in this moment.

This is why after twenty-five years in and around movements, whenever I hear the question, "How do I start a movement?" I think, "Where do you see yourself as best being able to serve humanity along with others?"

Reflection 🦋 noitɔɘꙆꙡɘЯ

- Do you think you have a collectivist orientation to leadership? Why or why not?

- Who are the key leaders and community groups and organizations that are part of your ecosystem?

- How do we listen to the whole in a way that allows us to make good decisions about what's most needed right now?

Calling ourselves in

I'm noticing a strong pattern, particularly among those of us on the left of things, to narrow the limits of whom we deem acceptable when times get tough. The political landscape has been bleak lately, and I've both seen and personally experienced a lot of reactivity born of fear. I've watched our tendency to circle in and draw lines of "safety" based on whose political analysis aligns, while rejecting those whose don't. I understand this as a way of feeling connected, but we can no longer afford to reinforce our belonging by shaming and "othering"—the cost is much too high. There is a lot of "us vs. them" going on, and I know that the only way forward is to expand the "us" so that eventually there is no "them."

I'm not judging myself or any of us for this pattern, but it certainly won't get us what so many of us are working toward—a world filled with clean air, water, economic and social well-being, and a welcome for every being. In order to move forward, we need to bravely work toward expanding "us," which can be difficult to do in such bifurcated times. It is so easy to slip into the pattern of delineating the "right" people from the "wrong" ones.

The U.S. Constitution is predicated on "We the people" and the Universal Declaration of Human Rights begins with an acknowledgment that "the inherent dignity and . . . the equal and inalienable rights of all members of the human family is the foundation of freedom, justice, and peace in the world." Neither of these documents says "some people." They say *all* people. These documents offer us exquisite foundations upon which to anchor our social movements, and although they have often been perverted, their inherent worth remains.

If we are to create a perfect union, then it is time for us to act accordingly. Not in a few years when the context has changed, but now. In this moment. Today. The polar bears, forests, and watersheds cannot wait as we pickily choose who we will call kin, while

rejecting and restricting those we do not. This restricting and rejecting is almost always done on moral grounds, and "we" are as guilty
of it as "they" are.

Let's interrupt this pattern and start again. Let us take a breath . . .

In a recent chat with some brilliant young leaders, one of them
offered the term "transformational unity." She spoke of the many
leaders in social movements who are working to create relationships
that transform and allow for possibilities not yet imagined. I believe
that this longing for authentic relationship exists in each human
heart, and each of us has the capacity to reach for it in every moment. I'm committed to remembering this.

This reach toward authentic relationship—wholeness—is often
interrupted by what we've learned about each other from our families and society. I know what I've been taught about the xxxxx,
yyyyy, and zzzzz communities, and my interactions with them are
colored (often corrupted) by that toxic load of lies and misinforma-
tion. It is our responsibility as leaders to honestly look at what we
each carry, and steadily work to clear away that internal rubbish.
If we are unwilling to do this, our attempts to reach across divides
and create reliable relationships is a farce—a politically correct mas-
querade that gets us, frankly, nowhere.

The gap between where we currently are and what we aspire to is
where transformation lies. Crossing that gap requires a leap of faith.
Being willing to leap—to authentically do the hard and excruciating
work of letting go of who we think "we" are, and reaching toward a
space with no "they," puts us in the realm of social transformation.
Carrying kindness and compassion in our backpacks can help.

We are almost there: in the large sweep of human history, the
days of patriarchy, supremacy, and oppression are swiftly draw-
ing to a close. It's like being at the oceanside—the tired old waves
can look quite fierce and scary as the fresh waves move toward the
shore. It is important that we keep our eyes and hearts on what is

coming in—it is precious, and deserves careful tending. We must also keep an eye on what is going out—it can be dangerous and merits tending as well.

How we transform is key to what we become. I invite us to relinquish old patterns of either/or and embrace the whole: messy, chaotic, and ultimately, deeply satisfying. I trust us and know that we can do this. It's the best and only thing to do.

Reflection

- How would your leadership shift if there were no "them"?
- Who could you choose to relate to that would expand your "we"?
- What are some possible risks if you did this?
- What are some possible gifts?

Joy

It's raining here in Oakland—a cause for deep celebration. We're in our fifth year of drought, and the rains are a gift in this very dry land.

This morning while driving, I noticed three people disembarking from a bus. They all had rain gear on, boots and jackets and hats, when suddenly one of them began to dance. Soon thereafter the other two also began to dance, so I stopped to watch. As I looked closer, I realized that they weren't dancing at all—they were gleefully stomping through puddles and grinning hugely.

I also noticed that they were adults with Down syndrome, and my heart soared.

When I was a young woman, I worked for a couple of years coordinating the local Special Olympics, and among my responsibilities was overseeing track and field events. Many kids with Down syndrome chose to compete as runners, and I got to know a number of athletes fairly well. I appreciated the frank and friendly way most of them met the world, as well as their lack of concern for the nuances and dynamics of race, class, or gender.

I also appreciated the struggles most of them faced living in a society with little room for difference and with a fear of and disregard for people with disabilities. Life could be rough on those kids, and yet most of them met the world with a lot of grace and goodwill.

A few years ago I began to notice that there are many fewer children with Down syndrome these days. Because of advances in genetic testing, parents can determine early in a pregnancy that the child has the marker for it. Many people choose to abort under these circumstances, and while I unabashedly support reproductive freedom and choice, over the years I've noticed the consequent lack of young ones with Down syndrome. Something that I'd learned to value and cherish is being lost to the world.

So I was doubly grateful to witness those folks dancing through puddles. They moved with graceful gracelessness and exuberant joy, one leading while the others followed. Another gift brought by the rain.

In the coming season, I wish you the simplest of joys. These past several years have been challenging for many of us, and most leaders I've talked to lately are tired.

May you have time to rest and play. May you connect with those you love and laugh a bunch. May you eat well and lend support to someone who needs a hand.

Reflection  noitɔɘﬂɘЯ

- When was the last time you jumped in a puddle?
- What might happen to your leadership if you did so?
- Who around you could use a little joy?

Bored of racism

Okay, I admit it. I'm bored. B-O-R-E-D. Bored. Of racism.

It used to interest me. I've worked to challenge it my whole life, and for many years I made my living doing "diversity" work. When I was younger it used to shock me, but lately it's been so ubiquitous, so pernicious, and so persistent that it's become ordinary. To quote Hannah Arendt, it just feels like more "banality of evil." There's really nothing fresh or new about racism.

When I heard about the incident involving two Virginia police officers, Joe Gutierrez and Daniel Crocker, pepper-spraying and pointing their guns at U.S. Army 2nd Lt. Caron Nazario during a traffic stop, my first reaction was, "Oh, again?"

While I was horrified by what happened, I was even more horrified that I registered the news as though shooting and killing Black people were "normal." While I understand my reaction as a way to ward off heartbreak (when I heard about Oscar Grant and Trayvon Martin, I was so devastated I could barely function), the fact that I was becoming "used to it" shocked me to my core.

I began to wonder why we are still behaving in ways that deny our humanity. What more could we possibly be learning that would justify lynching, the prison pipeline, or simple, everyday slights?

Fearing that I was alone in my exhaustion and boredom, I did a short survey of some leaders I know and asked: "What bores you about racism?" Here's a sampling of their responses:

- I'm bored that it is a new concept to people who have been around for a while.

- I'm bored that people of color are the only ones who "hold" it or talk about it consistently.

- I'm bored of its persistence—it's exhausting.

- I'm bored because we never move past the same old conversation, even though we know better by now.

- I'm bored because today looks a whole lot like it did fifty years ago.

- I'm bored by the lack of willingness to call racism racism.

- I'm bored of the "professionalizing" of racism—that there is only one "right" way to analyze/understand/talk about it with no room to fail.

I was struck by the fact that everyone had a ready answer to my question. My guess is that there are probably multitudes of us who are similarly bored and fatigued.

Why are humans still perpetrating something so horrific and hateful that it results in such a tremendous waste of precious life? Are we learning anything new? I don't think so. I think it continues to simply be a means to control/dominate/subjugate/colonize other humans based on the false distinctions of skin color. That's certainly not new. And our boredom and fatigue is part of what allows it to continue.

So what to do? What could have occurred such that the bullet that killed Breonna Taylor was never fired? How might we interrupt tired old worn-out patterns of racism?

The only answer I've been able to imagine is to focus on our collective kinship. What if Joe, Daniel, and Caron had recognized their (inevitable) common ancestor? What if they knew themselves as the cousins they most certainly are? What if Joe and Daniel, seeing Caron's need for a rear license plate, said to themselves, "We need to pull our cousin over because we want him to be safe"? What if Caron, on seeing the lights in his rearview mirror had said, "Oh, there are my uncles—they must want to see how I'm doing"? I can't be certain, but I imagine that the scenario might have had a vastly different outcome.

What if we refuse to see each other as anything other than the relatives we really are?

Clearly the situation around race in the United States is neither viable nor life-sustaining. Our historic and current ways of dealing with race are undoubtedly insufficient. What if we have been paying such exquisite attention to the intricate nuances of difference that we have lost the thread of our vast and common humanity? I wonder what might be possible if we were to spend the next fifty years paying equally exquisite attention to our common heart? What would the conversation about power sound like within the frame of kinship? There is a video from Love Has No Labels that reminds us that "Before anything else, we are all human."

I'm going to try on the practice of paying as much or more attention to kinship as I pay to the banality of everyday racism. This practice might not work, but the way of the past is not leading us to where I believe we are capable of going, and we need new paths and new ways.

Come along, if you're willing.

Reflection

- How would your leadership be affected if you saw those around you as kin?
- What is your current relationship to the "isms": race, class, gender, ability, and so on?
- What's your next step in doing your part to end racism?

Just say it already

In a meeting with my staff recently, at which Akaya was present, the conversation largely sounded like this:

"I just think that..."

"You know, like, maybe, if we could..."

Round and round they went, not getting anywhere.

Akaya stopped a woman on my staff in her tracks and said, "Can you say that clearer? What is it that you're asking for?"

Akaya's coaching was incredible and transformative in that moment. Watching her do that and model that for me, I asked myself, "Why do I tolerate the round and round and round and round?"

We tolerate it because we've been taught as women that it is a survival strategy, that if we speak directly to an issue, we girls get jammed for that. There are negative consequences to speaking forcefully, so we hear again and again:

"You're being so harsh."

"Be nice."

We learn to speak around our needs and what we perceive the group needs, and hopefully somebody's going to follow us so we get what we might want.

I don't know if I've ever heard a man say, "Can I ask a question here?"

Men ask questions. Women ask permission to ask a question.

✳   ✳   ✳

That's why I interrupted your staff person and asked her to start again. And even when she started again, she went around the corner to ask another question, and I redirected her to start again yet another time.

It's imperative that we bring those young ones along and demonstrate, in the kindest ways, "You don't have to ask permission for speaking your truth."

When we are rooted in deep care, concern, and interconnected-ness, and if we each trust and believe that we're coming from that place of strength and openness to learning rather than self-doubt and second guessing, then nothing we have to say will require authorization.

Reflection 🦋 Reflection

- When and why may it be easier to speak "around" an issue rather than addressing it head on?

- Are you someone who usually raises issues directly among your team or organization? Are there things that inhibit you from doing so? Or are there privileges that assist you in doing so?

Transitions modeled on nature

Transition is a natural part of every ecosystem. All of life cycles with endings and beginnings.

As leaders, so must we transition.

I learned this from Global Southern leaders around the world who I had a chance to work with for many years. They modeled for me that change is to be embraced, rather than resisted. Witnessing their triumphs and setbacks, achievements and wisdom, and their ever-renewing courage and joy made my end as executive director after nine years... natural.

I did not leave with a heavy heart, just love and appreciation for the intimacy we shared on our team. I left profoundly confident in my colleagues, who embodied our values in their work every day. I left knowing that with the support of our experienced and committed board of directors, they would continue to create and maintain partnerships that bring forth the best of collective action and embody the best of our humanity.

My departure was just another milestone in the long story of a more than thirty-year-old organization that has embraced learning as part of its fundamental ethos since its earliest days. I left the organization I led as a strong and vibrant organization, with a renewed and deepened strategy, and strong financial base—happily joining a circle of former leaders who continue to uphold and support the vision still today.

This leadership transition was natural because it was simply another expression of the positive, transformational energy emanating from the web of Indigenous, women, and youth leaders in the Global South. As in ecosystems, big changes send reverberations through all aspects of our lives. Yet with my leaving, the organization had a tremendous opportunity to expand the principle of interdependence—as living beings and as an organization—beyond its boundaries. As I left, I could only hope that I served such an extraordinary organization with accountability and care, and that I would take what I learned to continue to create spaces where people can connect with the universality of the human experience.

Inside or outside of the organization, whatever my role would become, I left trusting that I was part of a community that would continue to travel along a path of discovery, adding more context and depth to what we still share today as our vision for the generations to come.

I was there for more than nine years. It's only natural.

Reflection 🦋 noitɔɘʅɟɘЯ

- Leadership transitions are often assumed to be "trying" times for organizations. Why do you think this is?

- What is needed to ease leadership transitions and embrace them as "natural"?

PRACTICE

If you can, go outside in the next several days. Go somewhere with little or no concrete: the shore, a forest, or perhaps a city park. Bring a blanket to sit on, and if you're comfortable with it, take your shoes off.

Close your eyes, if you will, and notice the sounds around you. Breathe in the air—what do you smell? Is there sunlight warming your skin? A breeze on your cheek? Notice what it feels like to sit quietly on the earth.

If you sit long enough, you'll begin to notice that you're not alone. There is movement around you—what's causing it? Keep your eyes open for birds and insects, or waves, or the leaves fluttering in the wind. Perhaps there is a duck or a dog—notice that you are never in isolation when you're out in the natural world.

As you rest on the earth, notice your connection to all life. You are but a small and essential part of this circle of life—allow yourself to savor this, revel in it for a moment.

Imagine what might shift in your leadership if you brought this awareness into your everyday work. What might be possible if you were to commit to remembering this not just when you are in nature, but when you're in the boardroom, at a staff meeting, online, or with an investor or donor?

We invite you to get in touch with your connection to all life at least once a day for the next month (perhaps for the rest of your days). We're pretty sure this will deeply benefit your leadership.

CHAPTER 8

Flexibility, Creativity, and Adaptability

Many of the challenges humans are facing aren't new, but we've never faced them collectively, globally, and all at once. In many ways, we have never been here before. If we're going to transform the world we depend on, we're going to need new ways, radical imagination, and immense courage. No one of us can do this work alone, so we need bunches of partners to come along and join in. This gives us opportunities to try on new ideas, forge new paths, and experiment. Scary? Perhaps, but also replete with opportunities to reach into our most creative selves and make magic. How joyous is that?!

Learning from artists

> *What are you feeling?*
> *What is that feeling about?*
> *What does it have to do with your (life's) work?*

These are three inquiries that Sharon Bridgforth, one of my beloved mentors and friends, offers while guiding people through the creative process of art making, truth telling, and community building. These three questions for self-reflection bring us back, every time, to the present moment, from where all feels possible.

Through the gifts of presence, vulnerability, courage, and improvisation, Sharon Bridgforth and Dr. Omi Osun Joni L. Jones—accomplished interdisciplinary artists in the theatrical jazz aesthetic, scholars, and incredible humans that they are—accompanied our organization as artists-in-residence as we sought the transformative potential of witnessing each other in community.

We entered into this process with trepidation but also great excitement, for we knew something powerful was about to happen. By the third day of our workshop, Thousand Currents staff—every one of us—were performing deeply personal and intensely vulnerable works. Dance, spoken word, visual arts, narrative, performance—we laid our souls bare. Not just to each other, but to strangers.

To stop and consider that many of us did not consider ourselves "creatives," this was astounding to all of us! How did we get there?

Trust in ourselves and our bodies

We started through movement, so we could access the stored intelligence in our bodies, the wisdom that is beyond cerebral. Omi showed us that freeing the body helps free the spirit and we were invited to get inside of our brokenness.

"What did you discover?" Omi often asked after a particularly challenging exercise.

We discovered how fragmented our whole selves can be in this work of social change and how critically important it is to integrate ourselves if we are to do the demanding work of holistic social change.

"Your broken heart is the place of magic, of healing, of transformation," reminded Sharon.

To tell the truth, to dig deep, to go to sometimes dark or painful places, to craft personal experience into something one can share

—that is the source of art. This courage and this deeper connection to ourselves, our experiences, *our* stories, lays the groundwork for healing.

Trust in each other

Underneath so many conflicts is a longing for greater trust. One of our guiding principles in this creative process was to see each other anew, not just as colleagues but as whole persons, and be curious about each other as artists. In practicing that curiosity, there's deeper honesty, authenticity, and rigor because our egos had to melt.

Once our most intimate stories were shared, crafted, and performed, there was no going back to a defended way of living or working.

The process of opening ourselves up and holding the space for others' vulnerability—with generosity, non-judgment, and safety— enabled some innovative and introspective moments as we've been looking at our strategy and plans in new ways. Our staff meetings and planning sessions flowed easier. Even new staff who joined after the workshop were blown away with how much trust they found among their brave and loving colleagues.

Trust in the process

As a team, we fell in love with the creative process. We welcomed the call to experimentation with forms of expression other than the ones we know well. We crafted our drafts into authentic pieces of art and invited collaboration from each other.

Our artists-in-residence reminded us to stand inside our traditions/lineages but also as innovators in those traditions. Artists demonstrate to us that generating unity, deeper conversations, strategy, new initiatives, and meaningful collaboration from whatever is available is what can come from trusting the process.

Social change is fraught with uncertainty and ambiguity, but by "trusting the process," as we are reminded, we learn to learn, to show up, and to embody what we know to be true.

Joy

We discovered that this creative process, when we transform our greatest challenges into works of beauty, also generates great joy. This joy is liberating for the artist, as well as for the audience. Grief can co-exist with laughter. We celebrated each other through ritual, ceremony, performances, food, music, and dance.

Raising resources is not easy. Building alliances and deepening relationships takes time. At the same time, they are all sources of joy. If we emphasize the joy, we will move forward more creatively with our work, shedding the martyrdom sometimes inherent in our work.

Our artists-in-residence enabled us to commit and recommit to great joy in all we do, as a tribute to our partners, our ancestors, and to our collective strength.

Reflection

- How could you unleash your creativity?
- What wisdom does your broken heart hold for your leadership?

The long run

I'm getting a little impatient with how much time it's taking for humans to evolve. Really. It's not as though we don't know that everything is connected, that war and oppression are archaic and flawed, or that we can't trash the planet without deep consequences to ourselves. Many, many, many of us understand these things. It's not rocket science. This. Is. Not. News.

There are days when I want to run out of my office screaming, "WAKE UP!!!" Yep, I'm getting impatient. I'm utterly and completely bored of racism, hatefulness, littering, and all the rest of the raggedness in the world—there are days when I am not happy *at all*. I know I'm not alone.

And then there are days when I remember that evolution is not linear. Change doesn't happen all at once, and we've come a long way even in my lifetime. I live and work in ways that my mother could never have imagined. The air is cleaner now in California than when I was a child. I can marry whomever I choose in most states and some countries. These are big deals.

One of the challenges of being leaders in social transformation is balancing our desire to see immediate results from our work and having the patience to take a longer view. In some ways, change seems like it should be easy—we don't need anything to start acting with kindness and respect right this moment or repair broken relationships or feed those who are hungry. Literally—we can all volunteer to clean up a riverbank or pay just a little more so that workers at restaurants and fast-food joints can actually feed their own families. It's not like we are lacking in expertise or even commitment. What's taking so darn long?

Well, when I consider how long I sometimes take to learn a new lesson, I can have greater compassion for humans writ large. I'm sure that there have been many times when those who love me have wondered how long it was going to take me to learn a lesson that was clear to them and opaque to me. I'm grateful that my family and community had the patience to not give up on me when I was struggling to shift long-standing patterns that were impeding my capacity to grow. I could only evolve at the pace that was right for me at the time.

When I remember this, I can relax and let things take the time they need. The river will only go as fast as it does, despite my desperate paddling or remonstrating at the shore. No one of us is in charge of the pace of change, we are only in charge of our piece of it.

It's not about how far we get in a single day: what's important is that we keep moving in the direction of growth and connection. My impatience really doesn't help much. In fact, it doesn't help at all. So I'm going to work on being peaceful with what is. Right this moment. I'm going to breathe more and fuss less. I will keep working, even when the immediate results of my efforts are not clear to me. I will remember to come from a place of partnership and compassion. May you be well, may you be happy, and may you be at peace.

Reflection

- Each of us has a role to play in the long journey toward transformation. What's yours?

- What would you need in order to be at peace with what is?

Fly away stories

Late last spring, I was out in the garden, where there's a little cottage that is my office. It was a beautiful day, and I left the door open when I went to water the rosemary. When I returned to my office, I saw that a little sparrow had flown in and was fluttering against the window trying to get out. Since the windows were all closed, the only real way out was going to have to be through the door.

I went into the bathroom and picked up a towel. I paused and evoked my place of inner knowing, thinking, "Oh, my little sister needs some help."

As I walked back into my office the sparrow stilled and stopped beating against the window. I spoke to the little one and gently reached to take it in the towel. Carefully holding both sides, I walked to the door, released my grip, and the little bird simply took to the air.

This small exchange took my breath away—there was no danger between us. There wasn't any quivering or stress. In that moment, I realized that I had been told a false story that birds are inherently afraid of humans, that we don't know each other.

That story totally dissolved. I simply listened to the voice in me that said, "You need to lend a hand." And I did. It was so very simple: life helping life. That's all that was going on in that moment.

If I can center enough to be able to take my little sister bird out and free her, I certainly can try to offer that to the humans I encounter, given permission and courage.

And frankly, that is way scarier.

Reflection 🦋 noitɔɘʃɬɘЯ

- What stories have you been told or are you telling yourself that may not be true?

- When do you know you are in your "sweet zone" of inner knowing?

- Who could use your support in order to be free?

It's time to stop flailing

The "news" would have us twitchy—our attention snapping from one clickbait travesty to the next. I'm watching as we become like the dog with attention riveted on squirrels, waiting for the next one to capture our attention and waste our energy.

It is time to be rigorously on purpose and follow our truest heart. To clearly discern what each of us is here for. As leaders it is important that we become discerning in choosing where we spend our precious and limited time and attention. Let's follow those who speak truth to us and whose guidance we trust.

All of our outdated, archaic social structures have massive irreparable cracks in their foundations and are falling down around us. This destruction is loud and often compelling, and it is rightful that we witness, but don't get unnecessarily caught up in the manufactured drama that is not about us. We must be vigilant about where we direct our attention.

Beneath all the tumult, new ways are emerging. Can you feel them? They are right under the surface, ready to come to land—let's look and listen there. Let's attend to those energies. We may not yet see them, but they are fresh and bright and ready. Let us create a field of welcome for them.

Some of us can sense them in our dreams, others in prayer, contemplation, or wild dance. Others will hear them in the wind or in the call of the mountain or sea. There are myriad ways to listen in—please find your particular way and focus there.

The cacophony of dying systems will continue to be loud and distracting for a while yet: they have been thousands of years in the making, and it's going to take a minute before this dying is complete. But please know the paroxysms for what they are—death throes, neither bad nor evil, good nor righteous. They are merely dying, as all things must die in their rightful time.

Even as we may mourn what is passing, we can create room and spaciousness for what is coming—for it surely is. We can grieve and welcome, let go and bring in simultaneously.

Grieve and welcome, let go and bring in.

And breathe.

Reflection

- How do you sense when something new is emerging?
- What will you miss and perhaps grieve as new systems replace old?

Dancing

This morning I had a moment of deep existential vertigo. Everything seems off-kilter. Election fraud mythology, UFOs, mask-wearing as a moral issue, invasive cane toads, asteroids almost colliding with Earth...lions, tigers, bears—Oh my!

My daily newspaper reads like the *Weekly World News* these days. The voice of my long-dead grandma rises up through the ages to ask, "What in God's name are you all up to in there?" Frankly, I often have no idea. What *are* we up to these days? Sometimes it seems that I can't count on anything.

And then I notice that my heart continues to beat. I hear the laughter of my neighbors. The moon is full tonight. The waves of the bay lap against the shore. A colleague dies. A friend is pregnant. I remember the sound of my partner breathing (ever so quietly) as she slept beside me last night.

In a time of constantly shifting sands, good leadership requires that we become adept at dancing. We will need to become increasingly skilled in and comfortable with chaos and ambiguity. We can no longer depend on the structures that have supported the decaying systems that are swiftly crumbling before our eyes. We've never been here before, which is really good news.

How amazing is it that we get to lead in times like these? We have the honor and obligation to shepherd in a new and emerging age. How delightful is that?

We will need new tools, new ways of being. We will need to seek out new paths. We'll need to take unprecedented leaps of faith.

I imagine that many around us will be unsettled (we'll probably be pretty unsettled ourselves). We will need to count on more than our egos, our shiny plans, and our outdated traditions.

Part of our jobs as twenty-first-century leaders is to hold steady in trust that we'll collectively get through this time. That we won't

be the same when this transformation is complete. And that all is
as it should be.

So I've decided to count on the cycles of the moon, birth and
death, my partner's sweet and ever-so-quiet breathing, gentle
laughter, and the tides to get me through. And I will count on my
community.

Reflection

- What will you count on?
- Where can you find steadiness in this tumultuous time?
- What new dance moves might you need to learn?

Letting go, bringing in

Every year at each of the solstices, I scan my life and consider what I'd like to let go of and what I'd like to invoke. I find it's a good time to reflect on the past year and look toward the year ahead.

Letting go can be tricky—I can easily get attached to my ideas, habits, routines, stuff. It can be challenging to take stock and admit that I really don't need the absolutely cute painted pinecone given to me years ago by a child who is now in her forties. Yes, it's still meaningful, but it's dusty, I haven't looked at it since last winter solstice, and that woman probably has no recollection of creating it. It can go. I can take a picture of it in my heart and offer it to the fire.

Stuff is one thing, ideas are another. I can become quite enamored of a shiny new idea or project and letting go of it when the time is right can be much more difficult—especially when my ego is involved. Just because I was clever enough to have dreamed up something that worked, doesn't mean that it must last forever. All things have a lifespan, even ideas and dreams. Our task as leaders is to allow for natural waning and to let go when it is time.

Norma Wong, a brilliant Zen teacher, defines habits as unconscious patterns of behavior. She says that there are no "good" habits, because if we are on autopilot, if we aren't present and in-the-moment, then unconscious behaviors don't usually serve us. I think that's wise. So I've been looking at my daily life, waking up to the patterns that support my well-being, and am letting go of habits—my repetitious and unconscious behaviors. This has been harder than I imagined, but well worth the effort. I feel much more engaged and focused, and less willing to do things just because that's how I/we've always done them.

And then there are relationships. I've come to see that there is a rhythm and pattern to relationships as well. Sometimes it is time to let a relationship go or lie fallow. Doing this has nothing to do with its past value—it may just be time to turn our face or attention away from what may have consumed us but is no longer important. This is not to say that a person is no longer important, but our need for the particular kind of relationship we have had with them has shifted.

Letting go regularly is a good practice. It helps us to leave the past in the past and to move forward unburdened and clear. When I am unburdened and clear, it is that much easier to see what I want to bring into my life.

Which leads us to invoking. I love the process of imagining what's possible and then putting my heart and will toward it. This is where being clear about purpose and having a strong and compelling vision for one's life and work is helpful. Invoking, or bringing in, is a powerful leadership tool. I believe that the universe lines up behind us when we are aligned and committed and on purpose. It is much more likely that we'll get what we're wishing for when we're clear about what it is.

This season I'm invoking an end to war. I'm invoking peace in my beloved city of Oakland, in Afghanistan, in Palestine and Israel, and wherever people are taking up arms against one another. This means I am invoking peace in my heart. I now, publicly, refuse to be at war with anyone, including myself. I have a feeling that this invocation will take me places I can't now imagine, and I'll learn a lot. We'll see...

Reflection

- What, as we turn the season, is it time for you to let go of?
- What do you want to bring in?
- What could happen if you trusted more and controlled less?

Idea of a good time

I could be very successful as a singular entrepreneur, but it's not my idea of a good time. Even when I was between jobs, I've considered that my coaching or consulting business could grow rapidly.

It's just not what gives me joy.

The whole reason I chose social change work is to work with amazing people whose values align with mine. I'm a team person. I'm a group person. I'm an organized-groups-of-people person. That's where I do my best work, and where I feel the most seen, heard, and held as a person.

I haven't always built high-functioning teams. I've been part of teams where I felt overly responsible to make everything happen, where my staff were just executors of my grand vision.

Today I focus on surrounding myself with senior leaders who are really great at gently, kindly, and lovingly saying to me, "Okay boss, we appreciate you—and you're getting in the way."

These are leaders who know when to ask me and everyone else for input. They are also people who know that if I am staying up late, worrying about minutia, they're not actually getting the best of me, and so they will turn to me and say, "That stuff is keeping you up at night, tell us and let us handle it. It's not how we want to utilize your energy."

Other team members' leadership helps me learn how to surrender control. Culturally speaking, I also hold a belief that I have a lot to learn from other people.

Of course I've also learned that you can only surrender as a conscientious leader when you're surrounded by the right kind of teammates. You have to be able to trust that people aren't driving their own hidden agenda, and they actually do care about the whole as much as you do.

The world would be very different if I could do it all.

But what fun would that be?

Reflection 🦋 noitɔɘ⅃ɘЯ

- How do you gain confidence about your gifts and see the truths of your own limitations?

- How much do you trust the team members around you?

- What helps you surrender control?

Imagination

Our organizations and our movements are not lacking in vision. It's easy to share huge, dreamy visions for 2350, or whatever time it is when the rivers run free, everybody has full bellies, and the children sleep safely in their beds. Ashe. Amen.

We're also very good at strategizing for the next six months to a year.

What our strategies often lack is imagination—that space between vision and strategy, where we create ideas in our minds and where our desires actually live.

Part of the reason why leaders don't spend a lot of time in imagination is because we are so scared to get our hearts broken again. In that space of the imaginary, our work can become nebulous. It's where we must rely on what is unknowable and emergent—a place that is often unsettling.

Our broad goal and purpose as leaders creating change is to help move money in the direction of things we care about, toward values that we collectively have. There are all kinds of ways that can happen. We build spaces and relationships where everybody can have a say about how they're going to contribute to that transfer of financial resources. We have had to become more skilled at not knowing "how," instead creating the conditions for multiple options and choices to unfold.

Leaders build the culture and offer the space to be creative by the set of agreements we articulate, the relationships we build, and the values and common purpose we share. It's "easy" to write a vision or strategy, but creating a culture of goodwill and joy and excitement and unconditional positive regard among a group of people? Or ensuring a willingness to sit with really hard stuff and not have everything break down?

This is where leaders must plunge into the depth of their hearts and do their own internal healing work first. Doing the work means trusting yourself to listen to the whole of us, to listen to what's needed right now, and to make decisions that may make people uncomfortable.

Because when people trust a leader, they dare imagine something different. In the audacity of imagination, people become willing to say, "I don't know where she's going, but let's go with her."

Reflection 🦋 noitɔɘ⅃ɘЯ

- What feeds our need to know "how"?

- How do you create space and time to invite yourself and your team into the realm of imagination? Do you see this as a key part of your leadership? Why or why not?

PRACTICE

Gather some cardboard, markers, old magazines, glue, scissors, glitter, whatever you like. Set aside a couple of hours of your time—we're going to make a collage!

We'll use "delight" as the theme, so look for words and images that make your heart sing. Lay them out in front of you, and when you're ready, begin to paste them onto the cardboard. Turn your "thinking" mind off and allow yourself to play. Take your time—there is absolutely no need to rush.

When you're done, notice what it feels like to have created a picture of your heart's delight. Feel free to hang it in your office or a place where you will see it often. Imagine bringing this feeling to your everyday leadership.

How might your getting in touch with delight impact those who depend on your leadership? What might be possible if you led from a place of regular delight and joy?

CHAPTER 9

Taking Risks and Staying Steady

Dance happens between movement and stillness. Music happens between sound and silence. Leadership happens between action and reflection. The work of transformation often asks us to take great leaps of faith, and it is crucial that we are willing to occasionally take them. It is also crucial that we pause and reflect, so that we and those who depend on us can take a breath, rest, learn, and consider our next action. Paying attention to the rhythm of leaping and stillness, of voice and silence allows us to participate in wholeness—the dance and music of life. Therein lies joy.

Playing it safe

About a week ago I was in my car on my way home, and traveling toward me on the busy sidewalk was a young man (twenty-ish) on a skateboard. It took a moment for me to register that he had a toddler-age girl on his shoulders. Neither of them wore helmets or shin pads or any protection whatsoever.

My first thought was, "Stop! Get that child off his shoulders—they could both be killed if he hits a rock! This is child endangerment!"

All my alarms started clanging, and I was on *high* alert.

And then I noticed their faces. He wasn't going fast, but was moving smoothly and with expertise. He was also grinning from ear to ear, and the look on that baby's face was sheer and unadulterated joy. It's been a long time since I've witnessed such unselfconscious bliss. Their expressions took my breath away.

I pulled over for a moment, caught between abject fear and utter delight. My heart was pounding in outrage and the child in me was whooping in happiness. What a dilemma!

Reflecting on it later, I realized that leadership can often feel like that, especially when I'm taking a risk or trying a new skill. On one hand: "If I take this risk and fail, what could happen to me, to our community, the world!?" On the other: "How terrifically amazing might it be if..."

How often do we lead from a place of managing fear of possible disaster rather than going all-out on something that thrills our hearts? What are the consequences of this?

Please hear me: I'm not endorsing child endangerment or recklessness. But I am questioning what we lose when we listen overmuch to our own fears and the fears of those around us. There are many risks to take, but the greater risk is the choice we didn't attempt because of those fears. We risk missing out on the exhilaration and joy that is possible when we take a chance and leap into the unknown now and again.

These are unprecedented and changing times. We need new tools and ways of leading. We will need to take new risks, and undoubtedly, we'll fall down and stumble—perhaps even break a bone or two. While it's important that we're not reckless, it's equally important that we're not so cautious that we become moribund.

I'm going to push myself to be a little less "safe" and see what happens over the next several months. I invite you to join me in whatever way makes sense to you.

Reflection

- What is a risk you'd like to take that could strengthen your leadership?
- What might need to change in order for you to take that risk?
- What support will you need?

This moment is not the end of the story

We are smack in the middle of it. (Isn't that always the case?) What a shame it would be if we became disheartened now—that's exactly what those who are desperately clinging to dying and archaic patterns desire. I know that we are stronger than this.

Imagine what might have happened if Nanye-hi, Rosa, Cèsar, Ang, Martin, June, and the rest had decided that we hadn't gotten far enough and they had given up? Imagine what the world would be like if our ancestors who struggled to make a way out of no way had chosen to fold when things didn't go the way they expected.

I am leaning on the wisdom, love, determination, grit, and goodwill of those who came before me. They survived slavery, genocide, gynocide, colonization, and so much more. The least we can do is follow in their footsteps and refuse to give up. My father, who was born more than 100 years ago and who lived through harder times than any of us may know, would never, ever have imagined this day, and yet he never gave up.

We are on the brink of transformation, so I ask you to hold on—this is only a moment in time. Remember who you are and who you come from. Remember that our descendants are counting on us to be good ancestors. Let's keep our eyes and hearts on the next generations, the rivers, forests, mycelia, birds, and all who live on our beloved planet. They are counting on those of us who live now.

This is an amazing time to be alive—we cannot afford the privilege of despair. Keep faith, keep faith.

Breathe, hold on, and keep faith.

Reflection 🦋 Reflection

- Who do you honor among those who came before us?

- How do you want to be a good ancestor?

- What will be the next step you take in that direction?

Sacred/not sacred

Almost everything in an organization is ritual. We just don't acknowledge it as such.

Our regular staff meeting on Tuesday mornings from 9:00 to 10:30 is a ritual.

Patriarchal models of leadership rarely acknowledge that unconscious patterning is part of how tradition is established.

However, organizations deeply rooted in community often better understand the intentionality and purpose of decisions that impact everyone. These leaders can articulate a purpose for these weekly meetings: because Monday is for arriving back from the weekend, because Tuesday is not fully into the week, that makes Tuesday from 9:00 to 10:30 a good moment to reconnect with one another.

Although almost everything in an organization is ritual, all ritual is not sacred.

Often a new idea becomes a pattern and then a ritual or tradition. At one point, for someone, it was an innovation. Somebody said, "Let's try it this way." Then people responded, "Well, we don't do it that way. But...let's try it." And then maybe it worked. So then people said, "Let's do that again."

Next thing we know, five generations later it is sacred. As leaders we must pay attention to the pattern, because otherwise the pattern will ignore the people. This is how and why we end up with rituals like war or apartheid.

At Rockwood, I led an attempt to interrupt the pattern of consistent and unconscious overwork. Instituting a thirty-two-hour/four-day work week was our deliberate intent to do so. We were working with movement leaders at the time, and I was just watching people burn out. Burnout following burnout following burnout.

Because of our role in the ecosystem, I said to the team, "If we don't model a more balanced approach to work, then who will?" We had the privilege to experiment because unlike community organizers or first responders, we were not always in emergency mode. That gave us the space to "bet" that we could work fewer hours and become much more effective. My theory was that being more rested would be the first step to prove it, and we found it to be true.

We then had to set up new rituals and expectations around establishing very high standards of excellence. My line as the CEO to my staff was, "It's either excellent or it's janky." Though I'm not a person big on binaries, it was important to determine and articulate what excellence was to us, so that we knew when we had done enough. I have no interest in perfection (a mythical and toxic result of white supremacy) because the energy it takes to go from excellent to perfect is wasted. But if our work is not excellent, it's janky. And so we had to have a number of regular conversations over the years about "What do we mean by excellent now?" Our support for movement leaders meant we all understood we needed to be in a responsive relationship with them, and we needed to articulate each year exactly what that meant.

When people suggest to me, "We have to keep doing something because this is how the ancestors did it," I say, "Not so much." The ancestors were steadily iterating, trying, and learning, and so must we. Let us not get stuck in the hallowing of tradition, solely for tradition's sake.

Reflection

- What would happen if more of our organizations and movements saw themselves as deeply embedded in ritual?
- How does your organization, movement, initiative, group work toward wholeness?
- Do you make a distinction between fighting for others' rights and your own well-being? Why or why not?

Consistency + Congruence: A formula

What makes leaders trustworthy?

There are annals and libraries of theory and research at this point written about effective leadership, but far too little focuses on our reliability, what makes us steadfast.

We want to offer another formula for potent, grounded, movement-based leadership:

Consistency + Congruence = Trustworthiness

Consistency is about follow-up. It's about respect and love and care made real through our actions. Consistency is when those with whom we are in relationship feel and say things like

"You can always count on Akaya or Vini to come through."

"If she promises to connect you to a funder, she will do it."

"If she said, 'I will send you an email with the link,' we know she'll do that."

"Oh, she really cares about me."

Consistency builds trust as people know that they can count on your word.

There's also a consistency of being you, that is, congruence. Congruence is ensuring there's not a huge gap between what we say and espouse and how we move in the world. There's little pretense and no falseness.

The late John Lewis had a profound impact on us, as among the last of the venerated civil rights era leaders who actually believed in that spiritual organizing tenet of keeping the faith and living as if we're already there. Many leaders have encouraged us to make our own lives the unit of experimentation for the future we are creating.

Shashi Tyagi, an educator and social activist trained in Sarvodaya (a post-independence Gandhian social movement in India focused on self-determination and equality) was another such leader. When she arrived in the Thar Desert in northwest India the 1980s with her husband, they found deep poverty, illiteracy, substance abuse, intense living conditions in the desert, rampant discrimination against oppressed castes and women, and the purdah system, a physical seclusion of women from public life and the practice of the veil. They started visiting and surveying all community members on *padyathras,* long marches on foot, and Shashiji put her life on the line many times for her new vision based on equality, solidarity, and cooperation. The organization they founded, GRAVIS, has transformed the lives of more than 1.5 million people and still continues to grow. With a fierce spirit and steely determination, Shashiji always focused on building power. We lost Shashiji in 2020 but I am often reminded of the ways of being that she embodied: letting yourself be the first unit of change, modeling the ways that you expected others to behave, living your life with impeccable simplicity. She knew that to build trust in the community, her own practices had to be congruent with her espoused values.

We see this revolutionary ethos in young activists in the United States and around the world who aren't willing to bend themselves into a pretzel just to get a little bit of money. They are often Black and Indigenous leaders who expect people to "come correct," otherwise they will walk away from your resources.

It's been amazing to witness this transforming in our lifetimes, to see shifts from charity to solidarity. *That* is what congruence can do.

Reflection 🦋 noitɔɘʅʄɘЯ

- What consistency do you offer to your colleagues? Peers? Family members? Friends?

- Is there congruence between your external and internal persona, your public and personal life? Are there places or scenarios where you would like them to be more in sync? Who can support you in making them so?

- What do you think makes a leader trustworthy to the people they serve *and* to those who may hold more financial or political power?

We're all queer here

Being queer gives you freedom.

It has nothing to do with what your plumbing looks like or what or who you prefer to put your plumbing in relationship to.

It has everything to do with having more choices and privileges available to us. It has to do with ethos.

For many queer folks, biological families are not a given. So we find communities that help us survive, and hopefully even thrive. Without the hetero-patriarchy constrained ideas of having a husband or wife we are tethered to, or in our cases without having children to feed, we have been in positions—socially and financially— to follow our dreams. We were free to take the lower-paying jobs or take a risk if we wanted, knowing that our non-biological families would have our back and we would always have a place to land.

Queerness is not another bag of rocks on our back, but actually the place that helps us enact the greatest kind of freedom for ourselves and with and for others. In this freedom, there is much spaciousness to reimagine...everything. There's no script for how we *have to* do something or relate to ourselves or others. There are fewer "mainstream" assumptions we can rely upon. And this allows us to experiment with what it means to steward our relationships as whole and with intention. There's less room for "othering" and more acceptance of what most people would deem unconventional.

People can be and are queer without sleeping with people of the same sex and without being ambiguous or agnostic in their gender identity. Queer people are willing to be their own selves, to walk in the world on their own terms, to "own" their lives and their choices.

And don't we want this for everyone? Isn't that what liberation and leadership is all about?

We can start by having an assumption that everyone is queer unless proven otherwise.

I had hired a new director of communications, a cisgendered

white woman who was living in Washington, D.C., at the time. Our Operations Manager in our very West Coast office, a person who was trans and from Kentucky, was not too sure about her, her politics, her approach. So in one of my favorite exercises to facilitate, I paired the two of them to gaze into each others eyes for five minutes. Of course, their defenses melted and when I brought the group back together, I affirmed, "We are all queer here."

Years later, my new hire revealed to me that she felt that moment in her bones. Queer was not a label she was wearing, but there was no question that she was. She told me that my affirmation was deeply inclusive of her and that binding the team in the context of queerness felt deeply nurturing. It was a beautiful moment.

When it comes to freedom, we want to be the leaders letting people know that the party's over here.

Don't you want to be a part of it?

Because that's the only way we all get free.

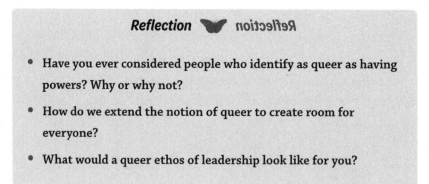

Reflection

- Have you ever considered people who identify as queer as having powers? Why or why not?

- How do we extend the notion of queer to create room for everyone?

- What would a queer ethos of leadership look like for you?

PRACTICE

Make a list of the things you regularly do. Pay bills, exercise, attend staff meetings, respond to emails, put kids to bed, seek funding, supervise staff, go to the market, whatever. Take your time and make a full list.

When you're done, notice the things that you do simply out of habit. Notice if you have any assumptions about how necessary they are. Are they? Are there any habitual patterns you want to reconsider?

Waking up to our unconscious patterning can be quite liberating: it frees up space and time for other things, like rest and play and joy. We encourage you to do this with a friend or colleague who can support you in your discernment.

CHAPTER 10

Learning to Care for Ourselves as We Care for Our Communities

We have a burnout crisis in the United States. Many people are leaving the workforce because of heartbreak, exhaustion, and overwork. This does not bode well for social justice. It means that after years of training up our best leaders in this work, we lose them before their work is complete. It is important that we learn to care for ourselves and our communities better. An orientation toward care and compassion for self is not simply a matter of an annual vacation, regular massage, or an extended sabbatical. It is in fact critical to cultivate habits that perpetuate joy in our work and keep us well and whole as humans. Learning to live in balance with ourselves, our families, our communities, and our work is essential to avert this burnout crisis. We need our leaders to be able to sustain themselves through the cycles of challenges ahead. Without the capacity to tend to ourselves, we will not be able to tend to those around us. We also cannot offer much from a place of emptiness. So this is an invitation to tend and care for yourself in order to extend the same care and love to others.

Impermanence

Everything changes. Life, traditions, cultures, leaders, cities, land, water...nothing is permanent.

And the reality is, we're not going to be here forever.

Knowing that—*remembering that*—can change our leadership because it allows us to see ourselves as completely dispensable: that we won't always be needed. It also makes it easier to live, easier to claim our joy every day.

If we release an attachment to our own lives, we can begin to understand that we are part of a vast, interconnected natural world that includes lineages of people who have come before us and those who will come after us.

Living dispensably also leads us to be very clear about our spheres of influence and to avoid falling prey to egoism, or conversely, apathy. We have to humbly realize that we cannot change or control everything. We have to understand exactly where and how we can make a difference and choose our actions very carefully.

Living dispensably helps us see that we have a relationship to power and that we can use that power for change. We know that the way things are right now—fundamentally unfair and unjust—are not the only way they can be.

One of the reasons leaders get stuck, angry, controlling, or co-opted as leaders—and cannot accept necessary changes—is that we're afraid of things changing, of something ending, of those we love leaving us, of ourselves dying. A part of us always asks, "What if it's too big a risk? What if I lose my house? What if I lose my friends?" Those are the things that drive us to not coloring too much outside the lines.

It's true that bigger risks can make you lose what you are attached to. Meanwhile, we are all part of systems that uphold the world in an unstable balance, and it's coming apart at the seams. And that's necessary, even as it is disproportionately affecting communities we care about or are a part of.

This can be so overwhelming, so complex. To not be overwrought and overwhelmed on a day-to-day basis means listening deeply to a voice inside of us that says, "Everything will be okay. Trust that fundamentally everything will be okay." Things will not be okay from a Pollyanna, let's-make-it-all-look-nice-for-appearances perspective, but in the belief that everything is happening for a reason.

Transformation is always possible when we consider that humans have been alive for such a small amount of time in the history of the Earth and the galaxies to which it's connected. From that viewpoint, elections, pandemics, and wars become almost trivial. It makes "winning the hearts and minds" of others perhaps not *so* important.

Everybody's dying. That's a given. It's also a gift.

So really it's a matter of: how do we want to live together?

Reflection

- How might knowing that we are all going to die shift the ways you lead?

- What if everything is fundamentally okay? What if there isn't a problem for us to solve? How does that free us to act boldly now?

Let's pay attention to what we're paying attention to

Systems of entrenched power do not simply fade and die. They become cruel and vicious in their fear of oblivion and often make tremendous amounts of noise. In a storm, the roar of the ocean is cacophonous not solely because the new waves arise and come to shore, but also because the old waves must give way and perish. Storms eventually pass—all things ultimately do.

Those of us rooting for and supporting these fresh new waves must not become distracted by the clamor of our dying systems. The death throes may be fascinating in their scope and cruelty, but ultimately that havoc is both ordinary and empty of any capacity for life.

Our old systems of supremacy are surely dying—all things do. I thank and honor those who are working to mitigate the damage the old waves are causing in their futile efforts to survive. I thank and honor those who have taken up the work of offering hospice to them as they die.

This is not the time to get sucked into the toxic, rot-ridden, decaying black hole of patriarchal white supremacy. It is not a good use of, nor does it deserve, our fascination or emotional energy. Pay attention, yes, but notice how much of the manufactured chaos is specifically designed to keep us off center, distracted, and edgy. Not worthy of our time.

Keep our eyes and hearts out for our kindred, even those we don't yet know. Watch and cheer the tide that is coming in—it is finally, finally reaching shore. We, and all those who came before us, have been waiting for and working toward this moment. It is arriving in a form we probably didn't expect, but here we are nonetheless. Look to the ones with bold hearts and exciting ideas and dreams—let them lead the way. It's time. Been time.

Let go with grace, mourn when we need to, and welcome what's emerging with awe and gladness. Yes, we will continue to be rocked and unsettled, but we can steady ourselves by remembering that we are inextricably connected to each other, to the earth, and to the astonishing web of all life.

For those of us midwifing what's coming, let's keep steady hearts and eyes on our true business: look to the young ones, look to one another.

Our ancestors prepared us for this moment, our descendants are counting on us, and their lives depend on what we do. Remember that we are not alone. Never have been, never will be.

We have everything we need.

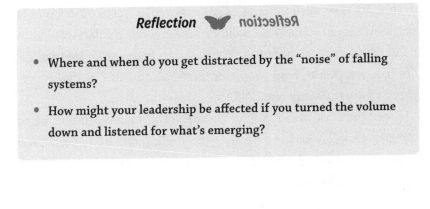

Reflection

- Where and when do you get distracted by the "noise" of falling systems?
- How might your leadership be affected if you turned the volume down and listened for what's emerging?

Pace, pause, and paradox

A piece of feedback I have consistently received throughout my career is that my pace is too intense. It's also a piece of feedback that I sometimes choose to reject.

For some, this feedback is about their reluctance to adapt to change. There are too many pivots. Others say, "It's so hard to keep up with her."

When I was a younger, more confused leader, I didn't take this feedback well. I thought there was something that needed to change about me or my vision. But today, I'm really clear who my pacing is for and why my organization exists.

In 2020, we moved millions of dollars to social justice movements so that we could actually consolidate an electoral win that would not hand democracy to the most extremist forces in the United States. I'm in a position to help people unleash billions, so I'm always prepared to move swiftly and boldly.

I love the slow, steady roll of partnership. However, if you asked our partners, "Would you rather get a million dollars in your bank account or do a deliberate planning process for a year with us?" the answer for them is clear. They'd say, "Give me the money, then we could do a deliberate process."

And so if my staff asks me, "Shouldn't we keep it small and create processes to really educate donors?" my response is, "The biggest education is for someone to have a million dollars less and know that they have helped with what the world needs."

So no, my pace is not the kind of frenetic pace that burns people out. It serves a purpose. I work hard to maintain my self-care and I do expect others to keep pace with me. We do this so that in our support of movement leaders, we can move fast and be nimble. It's intentional because our work is not built on knee-jerk reactions.

There are times when it's important to slow our roll, and my pace allows for my team to pause and reflect in those moments. Slowing down and taking a breath is necessary, but more importantly, when it happens, it's purposeful. It's for recalibration when things get tough or because we want to make sure that everybody is aligned.

So many reactive, unsustainable decisions made by leaders, ourselves included, are based in urgency, emergency panic, and without deliberation. Extending "I don't know" moments allows better decisions.

To pause and reflect with intentionality is a practice that must be cultivated within our bigger purpose, so that we can balance stillness and action—and still keep our pace steady.

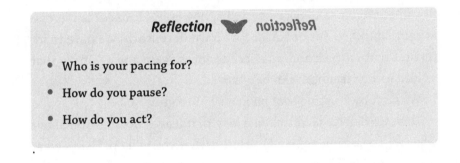

Reflection

- Who is your pacing for?
- How do you pause?
- How do you act?

Crisp and clear

We have gotten really, really good at having the "hard" conversation.

There's also something about direct, clear feedback that people can hear when they know it is offered with the intention to invite someone into their potential and bring them closer to what is needed from them. This means that we can say really hard, challenging things to one another, with a heart of compassion and generosity. Along the way, we have learned that the more direct and loving we are, the more people step up.

Kindness is a practice and we believe that humans are inherently born with the capacity for kindness. In a context of oppressive political, economic, and social systems, however, kindness is systematically squashed out of kids. So we have to re-learn. We have to interrupt that pattern and practice kindness again and again, so that as leaders our feedback can be received.

We start by trusting that people want to grow.

Then we deliver feedback in a way that leaves no question about what we are asking of people: "Here's what you will do. Here's what you will not do. Here's how I need you to show up."

We never know how this clarity will be received, but when we can trust that we are not offering the feedback out of our own self-interest or to tear someone down, we create the conditions for people's learning and transformation. We can keep their best interest, and ours, at the center of the conversations.

If people are doing the work on themselves, our feedback may affirm an inkling that there was something they needed to hear or have confirmed. When we get better at the difficult conversations, we create opportunities for people to make corrections or adjustments or ask for more help.

Genuine and timely feedback is too often an undervalued and overlooked part of creating the conditions for people to do their best work. If people do not react well to feedback, they may not yet be ready to make a change in their behaviors, habits, or approach. That can be disappointing but is also important information about other changes or support that may be needed on your team.

If we are grounded in ourselves, if we trust ourselves to be worthy leaders who care deeply about others, then our direct, clear feedback means that nothing spoken to another person will land as if it's there to harm them.

Reflection 🦋 Reflection

- When offering feedback, do you assess whether you are coming from a compassionate place or a desire to punish or penalize someone?

- How can you build your skills to offer corrective feedback?

Take a break from the noise

I've been reading a lot of newspapers lately, and it's messing with my emotional balance. Seems like all the news is hard: people doing terrible things to others, poverty, and violence beyond measure. It all feels quite bleak, and I've been carrying that bleakness with me.

And then I take a walk outside and see merchants with their wares, people going to work, delivery people going about their business, and bicyclists in their bright jackets whizzing along the street. When I really listen in, I realize that this town I love so very much is just fine. Yes, we have many troubles, and we also have so many more gifts. Our young people are poets and thinkers. We have beautiful public art that honors our ancestors, our museum is vibrant and reflects the city, and our food—what a joy, have mercy!

It is so easy to get lost in the story of degradation, to only attend to what's going wrong. Cynics thrive on this. It's not hip to notice what's working—too often we're so busy deconstructing the latest egregious act of the _____-industrial complex that we can miss much of the sweetness around us.

Yes, there was a break-in in my neighborhood last week. We also had an outdoor potluck and shared gardening tools. Someone's dog shat under my tree again, but my neighbor's annuals are in full glorious bloom. It's all true, and how I feel about my neighborhood has everything to do with what I'm choosing to see and attend to. Let's decide to choose joy whenever it presents itself.

I'm not foolish, so I lock my doors. And I'm extremely concerned with how many of our young men of color are dying in our streets. My heart breaks every time I hear of another life lost to violence. I don't want to paint a false picture of sweetness and light, but it's also true that Lake Merritt, one of Oakland's jewels, is being lovingly restored and is breathtakingly beautiful. I'm aware of social justice leaders working to change the story here in Oakland: creating systems of restorative justice, green jobs, dreaming up new immigration policy, and ensuring that domestic workers are treated with respect. So many wonderful things are happening daily, but I doubt I'll read about them in the daily news.

As a leader, how I show up and what I bring to my work each day has a strong impact on those around me. If I notice only what's wrong, that would have devastating consequences on the people with whom I work. I could see only the "good" things, and that would make me unreliable. To keep my heart and mind on what is marvelous about the leaders I support, while simultaneously acknowledging the raggedy parts, is a deep responsibility, and I've found it works best when I pay more attention to what people are doing well than what's not excellent. I've found that a four-to-one ratio is just about right.

What are *you* paying attention to? Leadership is about our impact on others, so I invite you to take a look around and notice the folks who depend on your leadership. I really believe that choosing happiness and joy is part of my responsibility as a leader and that the attitude I bring to every moment deeply impacts how people experience my leadership.

So maybe it's time to take a break from the news. The world will carry on just fine if we're not aware of every little awful event. Maybe it's time to go down to the lake or head to the museum or go hear some poets. I'll bet the people who depend on us would thank you for it.

Reflection

- What kind of "field" are you creating for those around you?

- Does something need adjusting?

- What might you pay attention to in order to create the world you desire?

- How might that transform the world around you?

Woolgathering

Lately it seems that I can't seem to organize my thoughts in my usual way. I feel fuzzy and sometimes it's hard to capture a specific word. I almost started to worry and then I realized that I could not remember the last time I'd been still, with nothing to do for more than fifteen minutes. I've been mesmerized by our pinball political frenzy, bouncing from an endless cycle of news and crisis and conjecture and angst.

This morning I had a chance to sit. To ponder and notice that the birds outside my bedroom window are singing in the spring. I stayed in bed savoring my coffee and letting my mind go on a wander. Truth be told, I felt a little guilty, certain there was something I needed to attend to: It's farmer's market morning! The dry-cleaning needs picking up! My library books are due! Emails to write!

I stopped.

And breathed.

And sat at my altar.

I realized that I've neglected a crucial aspect of a full and purposeful life. I've forgotten to create time to sit and stare into the middle distance. Time to daydream and follow wherever my heart/mind might take me. In the haste of moving from thought to thought, activity to activity, I've overlooked this most important part of life and community and leadership: time to center in and listen to the wind. To gather wool.

The other evening my neighbor was sitting out in her backyard with a glass of red wine. That's all she was doing—just sitting there peaceably. I was preparing dinner, and I glanced over occasionally wondering, "What is she doing, just sitting there? It's been at least half an hour! Surely she should be doing something—she's an active and busy woman!" And then it struck me—when was the last time I sat of an evening, simply enjoying the moment? I literally could not remember.

Our social change organizations and their leaders are suffering from a lack of unstructured time to pause and let life slowly unfold. Perhaps we should create something called "social resting." Imagine what might be possible if our leaders had enough rest and sufficient time to daydream... What could happen if those of us who make policy had abundant sleep every night? For those of us who are in the streets making change, imagine what could be possible if we insisted that the right to rest is a human right, and then held ourselves accountable for it.

We need us. We need our leaders to think clearly and dream the coming centuries. We need our work to slow down occasionally while we consider what might be best for everyone concerned— even those with whom we disagree. This takes time. And rest. And sitting out of an evening with a good glass.

It's almost spring. The days are growing noticeably longer here in the Northern Hemisphere. The little peach tree in my backyard is in bloom and the moon still makes her sweet dance in our evening skies. Let's slow down and listen to the wind and our thoughts and each other.

It will be good for each of us, for our movements, and for the world. Our great-grandchildren will surely thank us.

Reflection

- What is one thing you could do to slow down long enough to daydream?

- How might a little woolgathering support your leadership?

- When was the last time you gazed into the middle distance?

Rest and honor

All healing is generational healing.

My mother died of a very obscure cancer at the age of fifty-nine.

Before she died, I watched her work every single day, twenty-four/ seven. She was one of the "lucky" ones whose husband "allowed" her to work, so she worked a full-time job and single-handedly raised two kids. My father didn't see any of that as his job because he was a man, so she actually raised three children. She made sure he had food on his table, did his laundry, and the rest of it. When they divorced, she got nothing but the house and financial struggle. I paid some of her bills for a while because she needed me to.

My mother rarely rested. I can't remember her ever taking a nap, and that pains me. She was always on the move—working full time, leading the local NAACP and Urban League Guild, cooking, sewing. My mother worked that hard because her mother worked that hard, because her mother worked that hard, and so forth. I'm only two and a half generations from slavery. That's not much time. Many of my people literally died from overwork.

Activists and organizers often feel compelled to keep going—to "fight the fight" twenty-four/seven. We may think, "I can't stop. If I stop, something will fall apart!" We feel guilty if we aren't "on it" all the time...even when we try to rest or even when we sleep.

I made a commitment that if I am to continue my work for the long run, it is essential that I get enough sleep, rest when I'm tired, say no to things when I have higher priorities, and choose at every turn to *not* be in a frenzy. My ancestors struggled so that there would be a generation that didn't have to sacrifice themselves at the altar of overwork, and my commitment is one of the ways I try to honor them.

If I can break that chain in my lifetime, then it breaks the chain. I'm aware that when I get enough rest and exercise, it heals backward to those who came before me. If we can figure out how to live balanced lives, the pattern of choiceless activity dies.

This is very different from "self-care" language, which has become commodified and elitist. When I get a massage or take a rest, I'm deliberate about the "why" of it, which is not solely for my personal benefit. It is part of my responsibility as a leader to model not running myself into the ground, but it's also about taking care of my people: past, living, and future. I can choose to struggle or not, but I understand my attachment to struggle and overwork is a disrespect to all of the ancestors who worked so hard so that I would not have to. I'm committed to breaking that pattern so that the next generations can thrive.

Reflection

- What generational cycles in your family are you determined to interrupt?

- What cues or clues do you receive when you need to rest or take a break from work?

- Are you committed or attached to struggle? If so, how does it impede your ability to care for yourself and your people?

Trashy novel time

I've been reading less-than-edifying "literature" lately—books from the cotton-candy aisle at the library. I'm sure I should be reading some cutting-edge paper about leadership or the newest strategies for social innovation, but my eyes insist on seeking out post-apocalyptic science-fiction romantic space-operas.

Every once in a while I get a little embarrassed, and hope that no one who considers me to be wise sees what I'm reading. And then I realize that after many months of strong work, I need to step out for a moment and unhinge my mind. Reading, for me, is a surefire way of giving my mighty frontal lobe a rest.

Some folks eat doughnuts, watch baseball, or dabble in herbs. Others watch "reality" TV, dance wildly at the clubs, or get lost in TikTok-landia. What's true is that we as humans need to take breaks from our everyday lives. It's important that we occasionally step away from responsibility and simply play.

When I was young, we called it summer vacation. Even those of us who went to summer school knew that basically June, July, and August were intended to be months of respite from teachers and textbooks and tests. These were months for play and time away from routine.

As adults we rarely get opportunities for three months of respite. However, our need for play and escape still remains. Sometimes the best thing we can do as leaders is to snooze in the sun for a day or binge on salacious TV or paint our toenails multiple colors.

Our leadership is well served by allowing our minds to wander and fool around now and again. Think of it as "vitamin play." The gains might not be immediate, but over time and in the right "dosage," our health is improved. I believe that spending a bit of mindful time in Covey's Quadrant of Waste might be just what our leadership needs now and again.

In the coming months I encourage you to find time to unwind, take a breath, and do something that gives you some (perhaps guilty) pleasure. If you see me behind that novel with the lurid cover, come on over. I'll lend it to you when I'm done.

Reflection

- How might you play a little (or a lot)?
- What is your equivalent of a trashy novel?
- How might this be good for those around you?

Breathing and opening, softening and reaching

I've been wanting to curl up in a ball and cover my heart lately. The world feels especially cruel right now and particularly hard on folks of color.

I know that pulling in and shutting down is not the way we're going to get through hard times. The world is not well served when I close my heart.

So I'm breathing: remembering that I'm promised breath until the very last moment of my life. That's a gift. And I'm opening: remembering the many fine leaders who are working, nudging, cajoling, pushing, and pulling us as we collectively lurch and glide toward liberation. This is also a gift.

I'm softening: remembering that I'm intimately and inextricably embedded in a web of mycelia, clouds, newts, limestone, bison, and fire. All gifts. I'm reaching out, remembering that I'm never alone, even when it feels that way.

Transformation isn't linear and is rarely calm. The paths toward it bend and loop, and the way forward is often obscured, sometimes even by our tears.

Nonetheless, we travel on. We lead into spaces and places we have not yet explored, where the rules we were sure of may not apply. We risk and leap and sometimes fall. And if we pay sufficient attention, we learn.

In this turbulent time, I remind you to breathe. To open, soften, reach, and perhaps take the afternoon off. Let's remember that we are surrounded by gifts, not the least of which are each other. In fact, here are ten reasons to take the afternoon off:

1. It's good for you.

2. The sun is out, and the lake/mountain/river/park/forest/ ocean/backyard is calling.

3. You've been working hard.

4. Why the heck not?

5. The people who depend on your leadership will appreciate a calmer, happier you.

6. It's not the same as taking a whole day off—it's more like a "pick-me-up."

7. It would delight both your ancestors and those who will come after you.

8. It's been many years since you "played hooky."

9. Your leadership will be strengthened.

10. It's good for you and those around you.

Reflection

- **What objections come immediately to mind when you have the opportunity to take the afternoon off?**

- **How can you soften right now?**

We are all weary

I've been prickly lately, despite my commitment to generosity, patience, and kindness. I've had some trouble regulating my mood, and sometimes all I want to do is bite people who bother me. This is not how I want to live.

That said, I am living here, now, and the more I pay attention to this particular moment, the more I am affected by what is happening in the world. I am of the world, not simply watching it from afar.

About 400 years ago John Donne wrote "Each [one's] death diminishes me, / For I am involved in [humankind]. / Therefore, send not to know / for whom the bell tolls, / It tolls for thee." (Slight gender edits.) For those of us who are involved in humankind, it is impossible to not be affected by what's going on, and what's going on right now is hard.

So let's cut each other (and ourselves) a *lot* of slack—now and for the foreseeable future. The truth is that we will never return to what has been. Ever. We have no idea of what is ahead of us, despite the vast amount of prognosticating going on. Every single one of us is struggling to make meaning and use of this moment—if someone tells you otherwise they are lying.

This is a human moment, a global moment, and our descendants will probably look back on ours as a pivotal time—at least I hope they will. How we approach this moment will have ramifications way beyond the 2020s: let us pave a way such that our many-greats-grandchildren will thrive.

If we want them to be well, we must look for ways to be well now. If we want them to move at the pace of flowers rather than freeways, we must begin to live at that pace now. It is up to us, their ancestors, to make new DNA, otherwise they are doomed to replicate what we do today.

So I invite you to imagine a child in 2300. A child who is connected to you in some way and who will hear stories about you. Imagine: if you are to create a pathway such that they will exist and thrive, how will you live now? If you want them to tell a story of your life, what would it be?

I know that many of us are fragile and brittle. There is no shame in this. When we are asked how we are, many struggle to answer "fine, given circumstances." This is not true. Collectively, we are not fine. We simply aren't. This is not an individual flaw; it is a testament to our interconnectivity. I can't be well when you're not well. All of our wisdom traditions teach this.

So let's tell the truth and stop pretending. Let's stop judging those who aren't "coping" or keeping the status quo alive. If you're having a hard time, it's because we are all having a hard time. This is not about you, despite what "bootstrap patriarchy" would tell us.

Let's take a breath…and another. Take a break and rest if you possibly can. I know that not all of us are in a position to do so, but if we are, then do, and offer slack and support for those who cannot.

The world needs new ways of being human. It is time for us to evolve. I know that we have everything we need—all we lack is will and courage. We can't do any of this alone, but we can do this together: you do your piece and I promise to do mine. Remember that we are never truly alone—there are billions of us in this vast turning. We can do this. Of this I am completely sure.

Reflection

- **What might you shift today to create a path for those coming after us?**

- **Who can you reach out to so they know they are not alone?**

Yoga in the current moment

I am currently training to be an Iyengar yoga teacher, a tradition that comes from a very particular cultural context in India. I am learning in a studio where all my senior teachers are older white women. And I love my teachers. I have the same feeling of devotion and respect for them as I did for my dance teacher, growing up in India.

I'm studying with them because, in my opinion, they are the last holders of yogic wisdom in this country who actually put in the work for decades, humbled themselves, slept on mats inside a big auditorium to learn from the teachers in India, in a way that growing up my parents would say, "Man, you got to give it to these white people. They come to our country, spend six, nine months studying day in and day out." Nobody in my family was trying to be that uncomfortable.

So I feel a lot of love for my teachers. And every single day I have to navigate things like, "Vini, you know all the Sanskrit words, can you take a special class and teach us about Hindu mythology? Because then we'll understand yoga better."

I'm thinking, "First of all, yoga is not Hindu, and I'm Jain. Second of all, just no. And thirdly, I don't know about this mythology myself so I cannot teach you anything." As I understand it, the fundamental tenet of both Jainism and yoga is universality, their accessibility. The whole point of both belief/practice systems is to not be supremacist, to not be superior, to not believe in your own fabulousness, but to actually be available as a means to your own salvation.

Then I find myself on the phone with a mentee, a young queer Desi sister, describing this situation and she's like, "Oh my god, it must be so hard for you to be in like such an intense teacher training program, dealing with all these people trying to appropriate our culture."

I respond, "It's not our culture, baby. Let us be very clear. It is not our culture."

"What do you mean?"

"Sure, yoga came from India. But to say yoga is our culture is like saying tree hugging is white people culture. Yoga is not our culture. Yes, It came from our culture, but like most cultures, they are meant to expand. They are to grow. They're meant to bring people what they need. They gave us a sense of healing and belonging."

It's important to distinguish this because whether it's the dream-catcher on the car window, or the white guy rapping, or the Hindu-ologizing of yoga, where the claiming and adapting of others' traditions hurts our heart is when it becomes an extraction. It causes us pain when it becomes a way to claim a piece of you or me or an Indigenous person, or it's the perpetuation of making someone "the other."

With all of that to navigate, within a mainstream U.S. culture that is so focused on consumption, extraction, and exploitation, people of color necessarily become guarded and precious about our cultures.

So the person who comes to me and says, "Teach me about yourself by teaching me about Hindu gods" is making assumptions without actually wanting to know me. But my seventy-four-year-old white teacher who unabashedly says, "You can't cultivate a deeper practice because you're distracted," does not offend me. My teacher is inviting me into a better sense of self, with myself, and therefore, with the world. It's the intention. It's the purpose. She's not trying to consume me. She's not trying to prove her superiority. She's literally a teacher because she cares about my salvation and my liberation.

Reflection

- Who are your teachers?

- What cultural baggage do you carry?

- How do you cultivate an honest relationship with someone you consider a teacher or mentor across race, class, gender, age, and cultural differences?

Privilege the pause

One of my colleagues has just joined us from working in an institution where everybody was expected to be in all the meetings all the time, and then do any kind of thinking or writing or creative work on the weekends. She had become used to that as a norm.

For the first couple of months she worked with me, she would say things like, "I'll totally get you that report on Sunday night."

And I would respond, "No, you won't. You'll get me that report two weeks from now, on a Thursday. You have a child at home. You have a health condition."

I would watch her orientation to scheduling her work and meetings and would notice her making eight to ten check-ins with grantees who are all dealing with urgent security and protection needs. And I would respond, "Let's talk about secondary trauma."

Valuing our work by producing a lot is so prevalent under capitalism. Then throughout social good organizations we internalize it by saying to ourselves, "Thinking is a luxury. Feeling is a luxury. Processing trauma is a luxury. Being creative is a luxury."

This is the massive decolonization process of my own consciousness. There isn't one day in my life as a leader—in my morning coffee routine or in my long meditations or even in my dreams—that I don't realize something that's weighing on me internally, such as, "Did we handle that situation? Did I do the right thing?" Unless we as leaders, particularly Black and Brown women leaders, begin to honor thinking, feeling, healing, and creating as our birthright and as "real work" time, we will never be able to rid ourselves of the idea that we are here to make widgets for Massa.

So we have to reckon with our unsustainable and terrible patterns as individuals. As leaders we can no longer value our worth by how many meetings we're in, by how much time we're spending interacting with others, or by producing something for someone else's purposes. We almost never calculate in our work hours the time for reflection, evaluation, learning, reading, generating collaborations, sector building, or having a non-urgent but absolutely important conversation.

My friend recently observed, "You just don't grind on the weekends. I see you working really long and hard on the weekdays and then, like, you're out there sunbathing, drinking wine."

I shared with her, "It's taken me a long time. It's been a journey to not feel a sense of anxiety or guilt that I've dropped the ball on something."

There's always so much work, so here's what I am really trying to embody and model as a leader for my team: I have learned that after rest and play, I am 100% more productive, effective, useful, smarter, clearer. I have learned to show up in our staff meetings present, clear, and rested. I have learned that a decision made on Friday afternoon after a long week is not the same one I make on Monday morning. The decision I make on Monday morning will be a better one than the one made from a sense of depletion.

When we don't schedule our vacations or don't resist the temptation to plug in while we are away, then neither we nor our team members have to confront what is perpetuating the idea that we don't deserve rest, and that our unfatigued selves matter to our families, communities, organizations, and movements.

But we do. Give yourself permission to rest.

Reflection

- How and how often do you make commitments to rest and play?
- What or who supports you in your ability to keep pace with the work and set feasible goals?
- What gets in the way of allowing yourself to rest?

PRACTICE

Find a piece of paper and write a love letter to your
ancestors. Thank them for making your life possible. Tell
them of the lessons, both preferred and challenging, that
you've learned as a result of their lives. Please write this
letter from your heart and make it real.

Once it's written, place it in an unsealed envelope and let it
rest for three days.

On the fourth day, take out another piece of paper and
allow your ancestors to write a love letter back to you,
through you. Don't think too hard about this: let the
connection between you and those who have come before
you write the words.

Put that letter in an envelope and let it rest for three days.

At the end of the week, read the letters, letting yourself
feel the line that exists between you and your ancestors.
There might be some pain, but remember that these are
love letters.

If you choose to, you can exchange similar love letters
between you and the child you imagined who lives in the
future.

Remembering that we are all integral parts of a web of
humanity allows us to tend to our particular work, honor
the work of those who came before us, and celebrate the
work that will happen once we're gone.

It's Worth It

Joyful leadership is sorely needed in the world. There is only one you, and all of us need your unique contribution. Something would be missing if you weren't here, so we want to send you off with cheers and support.

A few reminders:

Risk joy. This probably goes against everything you've been taught—joy is such a silly thing to anchor leadership, isn't it? Shouldn't leadership be sourced in intellect, purpose, vision, commitment, and intention? Absolutely. It can also be sourced from joy, a place that is in the heart of every human and to which every human heart responds. Imagine coming to the end of your life and having those around you celebrating that you did amazing things and that you spread joy as you did them. Imagine being deeply satisfied with a life of solid leadership and contribution grounded in joy and connection. If our job as leaders is to bring everyone along and no one is easily dispensable, then exercising the discipline of kindness, compassion, and trust takes practice. There is joy in this practice and even greater joy in the results that arise.

Do your internal work. Discover your wounded places and do the work it takes to heal. When things are out of whack or aren't going well, ask yourself, "How am I contributing to this situation? What are my options here? What am I missing?" Interrupt your patterns regularly and skillfully and allow new lessons to emerge in their stead. Especially in times of uncertainty, we have to notice our patterns: Do you collapse? Do you flee? Belittle yourself or others? Please don't always come out swinging when things don't go the way you expect them to—anger is an important tool, but it can't be your only one. If possible, reach for kindness and connection when faced with uncertainty. There is much joy in forgiveness and redemption, not because these are the right things to do but because without them we simply cannot create the conditions for joyful exploration, collaboration, and experimentation.

Know where you're coming from, but don't get attached to the story you tell about it. Sometimes it's important that we question the stories we've been told about ourselves and our histories. Oppression is real but it can't be the only mirror we use to describe ourselves or our situations. Each of us comes from a lineage of work and survival, even those who seem to lead "charmed" lives solely based on privilege. Occasionally it is useful to lay our histories and our burdens down (thank you, Joy Harjo). There are many ways to interpret and tell stories about the past. There are equally as many ways to tell stories about the future and what may be coming. Notice your assumptions—they will surely be reflected in your leadership. A good part of a leader's job is to inspire others, and pessimism and fear rarely inspire folks. Know your stories and histories deeply and then release what no longer serves you. Don't let your history undo the joyful transformation that is unfolding in this uncertain present moment.

Honor the helpers and the teachers. Leaders can often feel isolated and alone, especially in moments of stress and overwhelm.

The truth is that leadership is inherently relational and there are folks who long to be in a relationship with you, to assist you on your journey, and to learn from you. Allow the teachers, the helpers to do their work with you—there are no awards or rewards for going it alone, especially in a hyper-connected yet uncertain world. Look for and acknowledge those who joyfully open doors for you, who are looking out for your best interests, who will walk this journey with you, and whose wisdom will guide you in these times. They are there—trust us, trust them. Ask for feedback when you are unsure, express what you're feeling about a situation, and allow folks you trust to interject, intervene, and help you shift any internal narratives and organizational patterns that are getting in your way. Engage in the joyful practices of keeping the circle whole and healthy.

Pay attention to spirit, dignity, inner knowing, and agency in yourself and others. Notice where you shine and where you have some learning to do. Keep your humility alive and well: that's the fertile ground from which we all grow and learn especially in these uncertain times. At the same time, avoid false humility: that is equally off-putting. Own your strengths—every leader has many. Nurture your inner knowing daily. There are many voices and pressures that distance us from our own knowing. There are many processes that rush us to perform. Be sure you are creating personal rituals to tap into your knowing. We do so by daily meditation and journaling practices. Find your ritual. When we uphold our own dignity in this way—and the dignity and agency of the people we are trying to lead, influence, or organize—we can have much greater impact that lasts long beyond our time in a leadership role.

Find your people. It's important to have people who can challenge our assumptions and patterns, but we need to be discerning about who is holding up and supporting our leadership and who is tearing us down. Find folks who are imaginative, optimistic, who are committed to principled, rigorous work, experimentation, and getting work done! If you're not among your people, find a way to leave. Honor your boundaries, especially when you sense that people are deliberately testing them. Be careful not to leave solely because you are uncomfortable or are unused to being in a new situation. Growth is rarely comfortable, so stay long enough to establish that a situation is truly toxic, and if it is, then pack your bags and go. There is no reward for martyring yourself when there is an abundance of people who love you.

Your people come in a variety of shapes, sizes, and formations. Too many leaders make work the only place where they interact and build meaningfully with people. Their lives then get fragmented between the people they work with and the people they enjoy. Seek to integrate all aspects of your life toward joy. Make sure you have spaces where you are seen and celebrated in your wholeness and not just for what you do.

Cultivate your capacity to imagine and dream. So many of our ideas, experiments, organizations, and social movements fail solely because we were afraid to dream big enough and settled for incremental shifts instead of bold and audacious new thinking. Sometimes we think small in order to avoid heartbreak—it's easier to reach for a sure thing rather than manage disappointment if we take a huge risk. Trying to control change rigidly is a waste of time in a fast-changing, uncertain world. Because we cannot see the future, humanity needs sparkling new thinking and courageous imaginings—it's time to experiment, to try new things, and sometimes we will fail. That's as it should be. That's how we learn. And yes, sometimes the cost of making mistakes is high, but mistakes are inevitable in the practice of courage, essential on the path toward joy.

Remember you are a part of a larger whole. Sometimes our concerns, challenges, problems, and worries can take over our day and our entire being. We can become preoccupied and distracted. We can veer toward the unique issues that confront us and lose track of the worldwide fabric of changemakers to which we belong. We are a small part of a vast ocean of life and are never, ever alone. Remembering that we are only a small and necessary part of a large and sometimes messy human family allows us to do our particular work—to do what is ours and only ours to do—and to let others do their particular work. There is a global movement underway that seeks a joyful and sustained way of leading. Maintain your perspective about your own importance and be courageous in joining this global movement.

Leading with joy in these uncertain times is an invitation to take bold risks, imagine widely, trust your instincts deeply, honor your people, remember to celebrate (and sometimes mourn), take big leaps of faith, and courageously join with others!

We are only just getting started.

From our hearts to yours,
Akaya and Rajasvini

✳ *LEADING WITH JOY*
DISCUSSION GUIDE

This discussion guide is for groups of people, organizational or community, institutional or networks.

1. Tell a story about a time you experienced joy at work or in community.

2. If we were to locate our collective work in a context of joy, what might be possible that is not possible otherwise? What is one step we might take to get us closer to that?

3. If joy is an orientation to the work, what resistance may we anticipate from those who are aligned with us? From those who question the need for joy in collective work?

4. How do joy and democracy connect in practice?

5. Given what we may practice, what is the future of leading with joy?

6. What stories do we want our great-great-grandchildren (or grandnephews and grandnieces) to tell about our contribution, if we incorporate joy in how we lead?

7. In what ways may leading with joy be transgressive and dangerous?

8. In a world filled with upheaval and uncertainty, is it naïve to veer toward joy?

9. In what way does this discussion itself create the conditions for joy? What are your insights about the meaning of joy?

10. Imagine organizations and social movements that are led by joyful people who are deeply connected to themselves, each other, and all life. Tell a story of such an organization or movement.

✸ ACKNOWLEDGMENTS

We want to acknowledge our loves, Kim Scala and Sayra Pinto, for your feedback, support, and encouragement in this entire process.

Thank you to Vineeta Bhansali for mothering us with meals, love, and demonstrating a life of tending to all beings.

Thank you to Barbara Jones for your steadfast sisterhood.

Thank you to Roveen and Vineer Bhansali for your loving brotherhood.

Thank you to the Berrett-Koehler Publishers team for your rigor and support.

Thank you to the New Universal for holding a community in which we can practice joy, for reflecting back to us what is possible.

Thank you to the Solidaire Network team and members for your courage and joyful commitment to collective liberation.

Thank you to the Rockwood Leadership Institute for supporting leaders making meaningful change all over the world.

Thank you to Thousand Currents for resourcing grassroots brilliance skillfully and consistently in the Global South.

Thank you to Jennifer Lentfer and Elizabeth Wilcox for helping us get started in writing this book. Thank you to Emily Doskow for cheering us on.

Thank you to Mzima Scadeng and Lucy Seligman for keeping us organized with such joy.

Thank you to Moses the cat for disorganizing us with your purring and love eyes.

We honor our teachers: Pearlene Adams, Mag Raj Bhansali, Umrao Bhansali, Sharon Bridgeforth, Marilyn Buck, Linda Burnham, Gary Chapman, Bhanwarlalji Dangi, Desmond D'Sa, Pregs Govender, Maria Estela Barco Huerta, June Jordan, D. S. Kothari, Prudence Nobantu Mabele, Herschelle Milford, Naomi Shihab Nye, Omi Osun, Joni L. Jones, Raul Salinas, Elvira Sanchez, Jorge Santiago, Heeralal Sharma, Paul Strasburg, Ana Sisnett, Prativa Subedi, Shashi Tyagi, Mary Lou Weprin, and so many others who lead the way with humility.

We honor the young folks in our lives: Ilka Arias, Tony Arias, Zane Bhansali, Kabir Bhansali, Keenan Bhansali, Kieran Bhansali, Ara Bhansali, Zara Ananda Bharadwaj, Nirali Devgan, Mira Devgan, Jiya Hikes, Michael Ludeke, Shannon Ludeke, Elyana Packwood, Corina Pinto, Sierra Shields, and Diego Warren-White for creating the world that makes it all worth it.

Thank you to Dimple Abhichandani, Maheisha Adams, Nwamaka Agbo, Romilda Avila, Nikhil Aziz, Gayatri Baisiwala, Maria Barron, Kelly Bates, Michael Bell, Sid Bijlani, Mia Birdsong, Nicole Boucher, Eileen Briggs, Andre Carothers, Rebekah Conrad, Sarah Crowell, Ashrita Daga, Helga Davis, Trishala Deb, Anirudh Devgan, Ruth Ellen, John Esterle, Maddie Flood, Robert Gass, Belma Gonzales, Pilar Gonzales, Pregs Govender, Crystal Hayling, Danny Hikes, Pia Infante, Chinue Igwe, Richa Jain, Rupal Jain, Cassius Johnson, Daniel Alexander Jones, Matt Kolan, Stacy Kono, Larry Kramer, Anisa Kumar, Marlena Lyons, Magogodi Makhene, Bill McKibben, Stephen Mittau, Charmaine Mercer, Bilen Mesfin, Maurice Mitchell,

Zohra Moosa, Mutombo M'Panya, Paula Morris, Pearl Fernandes Navin, Deb Nelson, Aisha Nyandoro, Liz Ogbu, Mary Owen, Tia Oros Peters, Damon Packwood, Swati Pande, Kamal Pandya, Sonja Perryman, Maria Poblet, Ai-Jen Poo, Susan Pritzker, Regan Pritzker, L. Ramki Ramakrishnan, Maria Ramos-Chertok, David Russell, Suchita Saxena, Maritza Schafer, Pamela Shifman, Lateefah Simon, Thenmozhi Soundarajan, Bill Stoddard, Dawn Surratt, Shiree Teng, Cybele Tomlinson, Onesiphorus Wambua, Jessica Wood, and Dan Zanes for making us wiser leaders and more loving humans.

✳ INDEX

Akaya Windwood facilitates transformation. She advises, trains, and consults on how change happens individually, organization- ally, and societally. She serves on the faculty of the Just Economy Institute, and is founder of the New Universal, which centers human wisdom in the wisdom of Brown women, and is Lead Advisor for Third Act. She was the President of Rockwood Leadership Institute for eleven years, and directs the Thriving Roots Fund, which sup- ports young women of color in becoming philanthropists based on generosity and interconnectedness. In 2018, Akaya was one of Conscious Company's 30 World Changing Women, and she has been a featured speaker at the Stanford Social Innovation Institute, the Aspen Institute, and the New Zealand Philanthropy Summit con- ferences. She received an Ella Award from the Ella Baker Center for Human Rights and received the 2020 Vision Award from Middlebury College. Akaya is deeply committed to working for a fair and equi- table global society while infusing a sense of purpose, delight, and wonder into everything we do. Akaya lives in Oakland, CA, where she reads science fiction, makes sauerkraut, and relishes growing enormous squashes in her garden.

Rajasvini Bhansali is currently the Executive Director of Solidaire Network, a community of donor organizers mobilizing critical resources to the frontlines of social justice. She is a passionate advocate for participatory grassroots-led power building and a lifelong student of social movements. In a wide-ranging career devoted to racial, economic, and climate justice, she has previously led an international public foundation that funds grassroots organizing in Asia, Africa, and Latin America; grown a national youth-development social enterprise; managed a public telecommunications infrastructure fund addressing the digital divide in the Southern United States; and worked as a community organizer, researcher, planner, policy analyst, and strategy consultant. Born and raised in India, Rajasvini earned a Master of Public Affairs from the LBJ School of Public Affairs at the University of Texas at Austin and a Bachelor of Astrophysics and Interdisciplinary Studies in Humanities and Social Sciences from the University of California, Berkeley. Rajasvini also spent several years working in rural Kenya with community leaders, an experience she credits as having inspired her to work to transform U.S. philanthropy. Rajasvini serves on many boards and teaches about solidarity as praxis and movement-building approaches to leadership through the University of Vermont's Master of Leadership for Sustainability program. She is also a published poet, essayist, popular educator, yoga instructor, and leadership coach. Rajasvini can be found napping in the garden and nesting with her family.

Berrett–Koehler
Publishers

Berrett-Koehler is an independent publisher dedicated to an ambitious mission: *Connecting people and ideas to create a world that works for all.*

Our publications span many formats, including print, digital, audio, and video. We also offer online resources, training, and gatherings. And we will continue expanding our products and services to advance our mission.

We believe that the solutions to the world's problems will come from all of us, working at all levels: in our society, in our organizations, and in our own lives. Our publications and resources offer pathways to creating a more just, equitable, and sustainable society. They help people make their organizations more humane, democratic, diverse, and effective (and we don't think there's any contradiction there). And they guide people in creating positive change in their own lives and aligning their personal practices with their aspirations for a better world.

And we strive to practice what we preach through what we call "The BK Way." At the core of this approach is *stewardship,* a deep sense of responsibility to administer the company for the benefit of all of our stakeholder groups, including authors, customers, employees, investors, service providers, sales partners, and the communities and environment around us. Everything we do is built around stewardship and our other core values of *quality, partnership, inclusion,* and *sustainability.*

This is why Berrett-Koehler is the first book publishing company to be both a B Corporation (a rigorous certification) and a benefit corporation (a for-profit legal status), which together require us to adhere to the highest standards for corporate, social, and environmental performance. And it is why we have instituted many pioneering practices (which you can learn about at www.bkconnection.com), including the Berrett-Koehler Constitution, the Bill of Rights and Responsibilities for BK Authors, and our unique Author Days.

We are grateful to our readers, authors, and other friends who are supporting our mission. We ask you to share with us examples of how BK publications and resources are making a difference in your lives, organizations, and communities at www.bkconnection.com/impact.

Dear reader,

Thank you for picking up this book and welcome to the worldwide BK community! You're joining a special group of people who have come together to create positive change in their lives, organizations, and communities.

What's BK all about?

Our mission is to connect people and ideas to create a world that works for all.

Why? Our communities, organizations, and lives get bogged down by old paradigms of self-interest, exclusion, hierarchy, and privilege. But we believe that can change. That's why we seek the leading experts on these challenges—and share their actionable ideas with you.

A welcome gift

To help you get started, we'd like to offer you a **free copy** of one of our bestselling ebooks:

www.bkconnection.com/welcome

When you claim your **free ebook**, you'll also be subscribed to our blog.

Our freshest insights

Access the best new tools and ideas for leaders at all levels on our blog at ideas.bkconnection.com.

Sincerely,

Your friends at Berrett-Koehler

Certified

Corporation